THE GRAND CONTRADICTION

THE GRAND CONTRADICTION

C. D. Davis

The Grand Contradiction
Published by New Wave Productions
Rogers, Arkansas

New Wave Productions, Inc.
P.O. Box 2456
Rogers, AR 72757-2456

ISBN-13: 9780997778106
ISBN 13-10: 0997778105

Contents

Preface

People have asked me, "Why write a book on apologetics?" I wrote *The Grand Contradiction* to dispel the prolonged misconception that Christian faith is unreasonable. If you've ever questioned the truthfulness of the Bible's testimony, know this: There's no good reason to reject God's Word. In fact, doubts are always based on logical fallacies.

The Grand Contradiction introduces a new way for Christians to defend their faith. Christian Apologetics, a branch of theology that studies reasons to believe, is usually preoccupied with the end result of reasoning (gathering evidence, refuting arguments, rehearsing talking points, etc.). This book offers a fresh, innovative approach, which focuses on how we all begin reasoning. The old line of thinking has fueled an inconclusive debate for over two thousand years. But this new way of apologetics decisively undercuts all doubts at their roots, leaving the Christian faith as the only logical alternative.

This ground-breaking book returns to the beginning of reasoning and discovers a huge philosophical problem. At the inception of knowledge, people contradict themselves. To start reasoning, people must break the very rules of reasoning they intend to follow. This peculiar event is what I call "the Grand Contradiction." Epistemology, a discipline in Western philosophy that studies how we gain knowledge, has wrestled with this problem for centuries, but to no avail. However, the new way of apologetics not only proves with sound logic the Bible's testimony is true. It also offers a solution to the greatest philosophical challenge facing our search for knowledge, the Grand Contradiction.

Sometimes writings on apologetics are dry and complicated. One of my goals for this book was to take a deep subject and make it easier to understand. I tried to stay away from a lot of the complex jargon you find in other works. I also included some personal stories and common examples to help simplify abstract concepts.

The Grand Contradiction was written for people from all walks of life. Specifically, I crafted this resource with the following groups in mind:

- Misinformed students - They're taught Christian faith is irrational when nothing could be further from the truth.
- Concerned parents - They're unsure how to cultivate a strong, thoughtful faith in their children.
- Church leaders - They desire a simple, relevant tool to equip the church for intellectual challenges.
- Those with doubts - They hear about reasons to reject the Bible when doubt is actually the least reasonable response to God's Word.
- Genuine truth seekers - They are inundated with so much noise, it's difficult to tell if their search for knowledge is headed in the right direction.

For those who wrestle with doubts, this book offers solace and instills confidence. Christians can now rest assured their faith is more reasonable than doubt. And nonreligious people can clearly see there are logical problems with their worldview.

Whoever you are, wherever you've been, *The Grand Contradiction* has an important message for you: Sound knowledge begins with God's Word. Any other perspective is based on a logical contradiction. And we all know contradictions are not the path to truth.

Introduction

Since the dawn of Western philosophy, a huge problem has challenged humanity's pursuit for knowledge. Most people aren't even aware of it. Philosophers have wrestled with it to no avail. No one has yet to resolve the greatest of our philosophical problems – until now.

Ancient Skeptics showed us that people begin reasoning with a contradiction. We all start reasoning with some basic assumptions about truth and reality. The problem here is we can't justify our assumptions the way our proven rules of reasoning require. Ironically, to begin our search for truth we must break the very rules of reasoning we intend to follow. This is what I call "the Grand Contradiction," the byproduct of a secular agenda for knowledge.

The solution has been with us all along. When people turn to Scripture and accept the Bible as their authority on all truth, the Grand Contradiction suddenly disappears. Only then can we avoid contradictions in our thinking and make perfect sense of the knowledge we know we have.

This book introduces a new way to do apologetics. It takes you on a journey back to the beginning of reasoning. There it explores how we might logically overcome the Grand Contradiction and form the most coherent worldview possible. By the end of this book, you will discover that Christian faith is more reasonable than doubt. Reason and revelation are in complete agreement on the matter.

Chapter one draws attention to the fact we begin our search for knowledge by making some assumptions about what's real and true. Assumptions are not the result of reasoning. Yet they guide our reasoning every step of the way. We can't directly judge our assumptions. But we can evaluate them by using the indirect method presented in this book.

Chapter two asks, "How should religion fit into our search for knowledge?" A scientific comparison of all our beliefs yields a powerful argument from analogy, which proves it's entirely reasonable to trust our religious experiences. Consequently, doubting the message of our religious intuitions is the most unreasonable response we could have.

Chapter three takes a closer look at our greatest philosophical problem, the Grand Contradiction, and asks, "What would it take to overcome this contradiction in our thinking?" Secular assumptions are the root cause of this logical fallacy. Thus, abandoning secular assumptions about truth and reality opens the door to sound knowledge (which is knowledge free from all inconsistencies and contradictions).

Chapter four focuses on the specific elements of a solution. Logic says we need supernatural faith in a special revelation along the lines of the Christian faith to resolve the Grand Contradiction and achieve sound knowledge. The history of Western science confirms this truth. Because modern science was founded on the revealed truths of Scripture. And since it seems science gives us sound knowledge, it logically follows that we must have a real, supernatural revelation grounding this knowledge.

Chapter five surveys the world's religions, searching for the best revelation to ground our knowledge without creating a contradiction in our thinking. By process of elimination, we learn Christianity is the only religion that offers us what we need to overcome the Grand Contradiction. Thus, Scripture is proven true by virtue of one simple fact. The Bible is the only sacred text that allows us to avoid the Grand Contradiction and make sense of the sound knowledge we know we have.

Chapter six outlines an example of a case for faith in Jesus Christ. Assumptions shade our interpretations of the evidence. However, if people begin with fair, open-minded assumptions (assumptions that allow for a solution to the Grand Contradiction), faith in Christ is entirely reasonable. And historical evidence confirms the Bible is that special revelation we must have to achieve our sound knowledge.

In the past, people have ignored the Grand Contradiction. Most philosophers and scientists gloss over the problem to get on with the business of science. But since when has ignoring problems led to truth? Instead of dismissing the Grand Contradiction, this book addresses the problem head-on. In the process, we discover God's Word is the best and only explanation for our sound knowledge.

The Grand Contradiction challenges us to indirectly evaluate our assumptions. And when we do, we learn one simple truth: Sound knowledge begins with God's Word. Logic, history, science and Scripture are all in complete agreement on the matter. Rejecting the Bible's testimony involves committing a host of logical fallacies (not the least of which is the Grand Contradiction). Only Christian faith resolves the Grand Contradiction and gives us a coherent way to make perfect sense of our shared human experience.

1

The Right Start

Right Assumptions Are Necessary For Sound Knowledge

BE MINDFUL OF YOUR START

A basketball game at the 2012 Hilton Invitational Tournament will go down in high school sports history as one of the most bizarre games of all time. The competition was fierce as the Blue Devils and the Knights traded baskets. In the final seconds, the Knights led by one point. To secure victory, the Knights simply had to inbound the ball and let the clock wind down. But something unexpected happened.

A Knight passed the ball to his teammate, seasoned senior Ryan Potocnik. Potocnik quickly drove toward the nearest basket and scored an uncontested layup. He raised his hands in victory, but the crowd was silent. Ryan immediately realized that something was terribly wrong.

What happened? This talented athlete ran toward the wrong rim. Potocnik scored the winning basket for his opponent!

What's most baffling about this game's ending is that Potocnik was probably the smartest player on the court. He was college-bound with a near perfect ACT score.

During a post-game interview, the intelligent student admitted he wasn't sure how he got turned around before the play. Potocnik laughed it off, telling a reporter, "You don't expect the smart kid on the team to make the dumbest play on the court."[1]

We can learn a lot from Ryan Potocnik. His mistake on the basketball court shows what often happens during our search for knowledge. It's extremely easy to begin a task the wrong way. But if we start off poorly, our best efforts are undermined. Just as skilled athletes can get turned around before a play, we can get turned around before we begin reasoning. And the slightest misdirection prior to reasoning keeps us from attaining truth.

Missteps as we begin our search for knowledge have nothing to do with IQ. Nor does a second-rate take-off necessarily reflect a person's character. A bad start is simply a matter of losing one's sense of direction. Just one mistake at the inception of knowledge leads to error. And once people are headed the wrong way, it's difficult for them to ever realize their reasoning has gone awry.

Aristotle once said, "Well begun is half done."[2] This is especially true when it comes to our pursuit for knowledge. The way we begin reasoning determines how good and trustworthy our results are. If we properly start the journey for truth, then our knowledge is sound. But if we begin with a false or unreasonable assumption, then we end up with a jumbled mess of incoherent conclusions. How we begin reasoning is the most important issue facing our search for knowledge.

ASSUMPTIONS

"You know what they say happens when you assume something?" my dad often asked me.

"Yes, dad," I reluctantly replied.

Crudely, he would snicker. "You make an 'ass' out of 'u' and 'me'!"

My father had a way with words. And although I would put it differently, he was definitely correct.

The Oxford Dictionary defines *assumption* as "A thing that is accepted as true or as certain to happen, without proof."[3] We all start our pursuit of knowledge by making some assumptions about what is real and true. These assumptions define what "knowledge" is and how we should go about getting it.

Assumptions are the most basic of all our beliefs. They are "foundational beliefs" as the philosophers call them. They aren't logical conclusions. We don't reach them after much deliberation. Instead, we form these beliefs by trusting our feelings about truth and reality. But this doesn't count against their value. On the contrary, we depend on many assumptions in order to live.

When we see a building in the distance, we assume it's not a mirage. When we remember time with a loved one, we assume these cherished memories really happened. Trusting our senses and our memories is essential for daily living. But we don't rely on these faculties because we have good arguments to do so.

Our very search for truth depends on some important assumptions. For example, we must assume knowledge is possible before we pursue knowledge. And we must assume that our rational faculties are valuable tools for understanding the world before we reason about anything. If we don't value what reason offers, then we have no reason to reason. As Friedrich Nietzsche put it, "The question of values is more fundamental than the question of certainty: the latter becomes serious only by presupposing that the value question has already been answered."[4]

There's no getting around it. We must begin reasoning with many assumptions about truth and reality. But there's an ever-present danger in our journey. Our assumptions might be wrong. And reason, a proven tool for establishing truth and avoiding falsehood, can't help us here. Reason is incapable of judging its own assumptions.

Even worse, if we happen to get just one assumption wrong, we end up believing foolish falsehoods. Examples from history consistently demonstrate this. The great astronomer Simon Newcomb reckoned the Wright Brothers would never fly. Sir Richard Woolley, an Astronomer Royal, insisted that space travel was nonsense. H.M. Warner of Warner Brothers thought talking actors would never replace silent movies. A quick look at the twentieth century reveals some brilliant people reaching bad conclusions because their assumptions about truth and reality were flawed.

Nevertheless, even though our assumptions could be wrong, we must still carry on confidently, as if they are correct. We can't directly prove our assumptions are true, but we must still trust them with unwavering certainty. Why? Because doubting our assumptions leads to insanity!

When driving around town, we don't ponder arguments about whether oncoming cars exist. When eating lunch with friends, we never demand evidence that our shared memories of the good times are accurate. If we dare doubt our assumptions, we cannot live a sane, healthy life.

Just try doubting your senses. Demand a proof that your memory is reliable. Such skepticism will drive you mad and get you no closer to truth. Worse than that, if we doubted our assumptions, we would never begin reasoning in the first place. To begin our journey toward knowledge, we must accept some beliefs as foundational truths, apart from supporting arguments and proofs. Making assumptions is an unavoidable fact of life.

REASON'S TRAVEL GUIDE

In the classic tale *Alice's Adventures in Wonderland*, Alice stumbles down a rabbit hole and finds herself in a strange world. During her wanderings, she encounters a grinning Cheshire Cat. Alice asks the cat, "Would you tell me, please, which way I ought to go from here?"

"That depends a good deal on where you want to get to," the curious feline responds. [5]

Alice's conversation with the Cheshire Cat sheds light on how our assumptions guide our reasoning. We often think of reason as if it were an objective practice, a scale to impartially weight evidence. We turn to logic and science, asking the simple question "What is knowledge?" But in reality, our assumptions have already answered that question.

When we make assumptions about truth and reality, we instantly set an agenda for reason. We mark out a course for the sciences. We decide where philosophy will take us. In short, we set the boundaries for knowledge. And all this happens before we ever begin reasoning. Assumptions are reason's travel guide, taking us in a direction we have already determined.

Plato proved as much in his *Meno*. A man named Meno once asked Socrates, "How can you inquire about what you don't already know?"[6] This silly question makes a profound point. We must know (that is, assume) something about what we are looking for before we can ever hope to find it. For example, if my neighbor lost his dog, I must first know what his dog looks like in order to search for it. Similarly, we all must have a basic idea about what knowledge is, what is real and true, before we can get down to the business of seeking after it. And it's our assumptions that ultimately decide what we are looking for.

SELF-CHECKING

When I was in high school, the football coach was my history teacher. He gave the class weekly quizzes and then let us students grade our own tests! Somehow everyone in the class earned high marks. The downside of this self-checking was that we didn't really learn much.

Thinking about assumptions reminds me of this class. My classmates had a variety of opinions. And they tested their conclusions by grading their own work. At the end of the year, they didn't have much knowledge to show for it. Philosophers do this sort of self-checking all the time. Does it lead to truth?

Western philosophy is filled with a number of different assumptions about knowledge. Empiricists, rationalists, existentialists and skeptics all have their own opinions about what knowledge is and how to go about getting it. Because of their different assumptions, they draw different conclusions. But which of the philosophers are correct? Which group begins with the best assumptions?

It's easy to say, "Let's evaluate our assumptions." But this task is actually quite difficult. Judging our assumptions is like grading our own schoolwork. Naturally, we are going to give ourselves a good score. And why not? We already believe our assumptions are correct; otherwise, they wouldn't be our assumptions in the first place.

Sadly, we are unable to directly judge our assumptions. Why? Because our very reasoning already depends on them. We believe our assumptions are true before we ever start thinking about our assumptions. Because of this situation, objectively self-checking assumptions is a very difficult task.

ROUND AND ROUND

We have a far greater problem with evaluating our assumptions. The moment we consider their truthfulness, we force ourselves to commit a number of logical fallacies. The most condemning of these is circular reasoning.

Aristotle set an enduring standard when he established the rule *against* circular reasoning. "A circular demonstration is no demonstration at all," Aristotle maintained.[7] This proven rule of reasoning has stood the test of time. Its value to our search for truth is impossible to deny.

Circular reasoning occurs when the conclusion of a logical argument is also a premise within the argument. In general, if someone says, "A is true because B is true; B is true because A is true," he or she is reasoning in a circle. This practice is clearly not the way to knowledge. If we allow someone to reason in a circle, then he or she can pretty much "prove" anything. Most philosophers regard circular reasoning as the worst of logical fallacies.

To give you an example of how absurd circular reasoning is, let me explain my wife's attitude toward couponing. When my wife receives a coupon in the mail, she quickly redeems it at the clothing store. She returns home, holds up her new dress, and says, "Look! I saved twenty dollars today!" On the surface, this sounds great. However, once I find out that she used a twenty-percent-off coupon to buy a one hundred-dollar dress, I respond, "You didn't save twenty dollars. You spent eighty dollars!"

I never win this argument with my wife, but her couponing logic is still a great example of circular reasoning. Can you see how my wife's coupon is a good thing only if she first assumes she needs a new wardrobe? My wife finds a coupon and interprets it as a great reason to go shopping. I see coupons as a marketing ploy by big corporations. My wife and I definitely have different assumptions about her clothing needs. My wife assumes she needs more dresses. I assume she has enough.

My wife's argument to justify her shopping looks something like this:

Premise 1: I need to go shopping.
Premise 2: I received a coupon.
Conclusion: Therefore, I need to go shopping.

Notice that premise 1 and the conclusion are the same. This argument is circular because the conclusion is also a premise. My wife concluded "I need to go shopping" only because she first assumed she needs to go shopping. This is "begging the question" (as the philosophers say) and reasoning in a circle. As you can see, the conclusion is just a restatement of what she already believes. And reasoning circularly never gets us any closer to the truth.

This is exactly what happens when we try to directly judge our assumptions. How could we argue for our assumptions when we must depend upon them in order to do so? We can't very well reason about our assumptions when our reasoning is based on the very assumptions in question. Take, for example, the assumption "My senses are reliable." We can't give a valid argument for our senses when somewhere within the argument we must refer to our senses as if they are, in fact, reliable. This is nothing more than circular reasoning.

This is the greatest problem we face when we try to directly judge the truthfulness of any of our assumptions. If we argue for an assumption in a simple, straightforward manner, we are merely reasoning in a circle. Sadly, reason has little to offer us in this respect.

THE ORIGIN OF ASSUMPTIONS

My daughter's birth was one of the greatest moments in my life. I can vividly remember the moment in the delivery room when I heard my newborn child cry for the first time. To this day, I still view the birth of my child as a wonderful mystery. Sure, scientists can observe through a microscope how sperm fertilizes an egg. They can explain cellular division within an embryo. But doctors still can't pinpoint with certainty the precise moment when life begins. Nor can they fully explain why the birthing process unfolds as it does.

There is still much mystery behind the glimpse into reality that science offers. Science aptly understands the mechanics, the "how," of nature. But scientists are unable to address "why" nature operates as it does. Even though scientists know a great deal about biology, the ultimate causes behind the birth of a child are still a mystery.

This mystery behind my daughter's birth is similar to the mystery shrouding our assumptions. We find ourselves trusting our assumptions with the greatest certainty, depending upon them at every turn. But we don't know exactly where they come from. Some philosophers say our assumptions are based on natural instincts. Others say they are caused by supernatural intuitions. Despite these disagreements, we all can agree on one thing. We have curious feelings that compel us to believe in our most basic truths.

We can only speculate about what causes us to feel the things we do about truth and reality. All we reasonably know is that assumptions are not the product of logical reasoning. We don't trust our senses because of a good argument. Nor do we take our memories as accurate because of a scientific experiment. As Blaise Pascal said, "We know our first principles in a way which reason has no part of."[8]

There is always a degree of mystery behind our knowledge. Even the greatest intellectual foe of the Christian faith, David Hume, admitted as much when he wrote, "No philosopher, who is rational and modest, has ever pretended to know the ultimate cause behind any natural operation. Science merely staves off our ignorance a little longer."[9]

The most we can confidently say about our assumptions is that subtle, involuntary feelings compel us to hold on to our basic beliefs about what is real and true. We trust our assumptions with absolute certainty even though we have no arguments for them. We trust them because of our feelings. And concerning the cause of these feelings, we must admit ignorance.

THE SKEPTIC'S COMPLAINT

By now you can see the challenge assumptions pose to our search for knowledge. We begin reasoning by making a number of assumptions about what is real and true. We can't reasonably prove they are correct, but we must trust them anyway. We feel they are certain, but we aren't sure why. And what's most concerning is these assumptions guide every step of our reasoning.

This entire situation is unnerving for truth seekers who look to human reason for answers. The Skeptics of Western philosophy were troubled by all this. They understood that we must begin reasoning with the right assumptions to attain truth. They wrestled with these concerns and came to an absurd conclusion. They insisted knowledge is impossible. Ironically, they spoke as if they knew such a thing.

The Skeptics made a judgment to make no judgments. In the end, they couldn't practice what they preached. A consistent skeptic would doubt all of his or her assumptions and consequently he or she would never begin reasoning. A real skeptic could not live a sane life. As Aristotle said, "A true skeptic would be a vegetable, unable to move or even speak."[10]

Despite all their contradictions, ancient Skeptics taught us one positive thing. We must make sure to get our assumptions right before we begin reasoning. It's crucial for us to start our pursuit for knowledge with the proper assumptions.

But this task is much harder than it sounds. The Skeptics asked a simple question, "How do you know your assumptions are true?" They never discovered a satisfactory answer. Finally, they gave up on their pursuit for knowledge.

Other philosophers fared no better. Most simply glossed over questions dealing with their assumptions to get on with the business of philosophy. Scientists ignored problems with their assumptions so they could understand the world as they saw fit. But how can suppressing questions lead to truth? Since when has ignoring our problems been a path to knowledge? The Skeptics' original question is still unanswered. And all the age-old problems that come along with assuming are still there.

To the point, secular philosophy and modern science are based on the basic assumption "Knowledge is only about physical things we can see and touch." Secularists reject the thought of religion, branding it as useless superstition. They assume "truth" is something equally accessible by all, reached solely through the senses. But why should anyone assume this? It isn't evident from sight alone that sight alone is the only way to truth. Nor does everyone believe "Everyone must believe something if it's true."

The most common secular assumptions about knowledge are problematic not just because they are arbitrary and without good supporting reasons. Secular assumptions can't even live up to their own self-imposed truth standards. They don't pass their own rational tests! Something is clearly amiss here.

THE PROPHET'S SOLUTION

In the early days of Western philosophy, the Skeptics wandered the streets of Greece, questioning everyone's assumptions about truth and reality. Little did they know, the answers to all their questions could be found across the Mediterranean Sea. Some two hundred years before the birth of Western philosophy, Israel's prophets offered sound solutions to all the philosophers' nagging questions.

The prophets of God insisted we must base our reasoning on something other than human thoughts about physical things. When we begin with natural human thoughts, we always start off with inconsistencies. Reason says, "We must back our beliefs with sound arguments," but we have no sound argument for the beliefs that matter most (our assumptions). Reason calls us to justify our actions with good, noncircular reasons. But we haven't a good, noncircular reason to begin reasoning in the first place. These problems at the root of human reasoning lead us to build knowledge on top of inconsistencies and logical fallacies.

To avoid this dilemma, we need to begin our search for knowledge with something greater than what the human mind can give. We require basic truths beyond what common reasoning can offer. Only then can reasoning begin properly. In short, we need something outside ourselves and our world, a source of knowledge greater than human reasoning, in order to overcome all the problems surrounding the inception of knowledge.

Israel's prophets proclaimed that we must take God's Word, the Bible, as our absolute authority on all truth. And this must occur at the very beginning of our journey. Otherwise, our pursuit for truth is thwarted. Jeremiah cried out, "The wise have trapped themselves so long as they reject the Word of the LORD!" (8:9). And Isaiah warned, "The LORD turns the knowledge of the wise into foolishness!" (44:25). The basic message of the prophets was simple. Sound knowledge begins with God's Word. If we don't base our reasoning on God's revealed truths, our search for knowledge encounters many self-defeating problems. Thus, David's song rings true, "Only a fool has said in his heart, 'There is no God'" (Ps. 14:1).

This might sound odd to say. It might come across as silly, even superstitious to the modern mind. But why should we so quickly react to God's Word with cynicism? Perhaps in our youth, our parents or teachers encouraged us to slight religion. Maybe our friends aren't religious. Or our culture promotes a secular lifestyle. Doubt might even be fueled by emotional responses to life's disappointments. Whatever is behind a person's doubts, know this: Doubt is never based on sound reasoning.

The things that lead a person to reject the Bible's testimony might be persuasive, but they surely aren't rational. They are what the philosophers call "informal logical fallacies." Appeals to another person's authority, to popular opinions, to emotional reactions and to personal desires are all illogical. Time and time again, these things prove themselves unreasonable. Clearly, logical fallacies are not the way to truth. But these are precisely the things that persuade people to doubt both God's existence and God's revelations to humanity.

Strictly speaking, nothing is inherently unreasonable about trusting the Bible. Its teachings are logically possible, meaning there's no contradiction in the thought of the marvels recorded in Scripture. Nor does our human experience necessarily speak against such supernatural realities. Everything that happens in our lives can be explained religiously. And biblical teachings that appear inconsistent on the surface are easily reconciled with the proper assumptions.

Furthermore, Western science is (or can be) in full agreement with God's Word. Even if evolutionary theory turned out to be undeniable, this still wouldn't count against faith. God could have easily used evolution to create life in six figurative "days" (that is, six extended periods of time). The biblical stories of Adam and Eve aren't necessarily historical. Obviously, people with different assumptions interpret the creation account differently. But the fact is this: Absolutely nothing from reason or experience necessarily conflicts with the teachings of Scripture. If they happen to clash, then a simple revision of one's assumptions easily resolves the tension.

Given all this, it's hard to say why ancient Greece didn't look to Israel's prophets for answers. Whatever the reason, it certainly wasn't reasonable. Sure, if someone assumes "God can't communicate with us," "Miracles never happen," or "God doesn't exist," then the thought of a prophet seems absurd. If someone assumes "Knowledge is only about physical things" or "Reason has nothing to do with religion," then faith appears completely irrational. With secular assumptions like these, it's easy to see how secularists reach conclusions like "The Bible is a book of fables" and "Jesus was just your average man."

But all this really demonstrates is secular assumptions lead to secular conclusions. The paramount question still remains, "Why think secular assumptions are true?" This is the most important question we must ask while searching for knowledge.

INDIRECT TESTS

Christopher Columbus sailed across the Atlantic Ocean and eventually discovered America. Did you ever wonder how he made it? When sailors navigated the open seas, they calculated their position using a method called dead reckoning. Sailors measured their speed, observed their course and periodically plotted their position on a map.

Dead reckoning was a useful tool, but it was subject to error. Factors like the wind and waves constantly altered a ship's course and speed. Because navigators plotted their new location based on the last known location, the slightest error had a cumulative effect on one's journey. A fractional mistake at the beginning of a trip led to a huge error at the end.

If sailors were thrown off course, they wouldn't realize it until they stopped their calculations, put down their drawings and looked around at their surroundings. And when they saw land earlier than expected, all the past mistakes suddenly became apparent. Navigating errors were often discovered in spite of a sailor's calculations, not because of them.

Dead reckoning resembles how we must navigate our search for knowledge. We reason about newer beliefs based on older convictions. If we happen to veer off course—if an older belief (or assumption) is wrong—it's difficult to recognize the error of our ways. So, we must stop reasoning for a moment and question everything we once thought was true. Simply put, we must question our assumptions.

Although we can't directly judge an assumption, we can still ask ourselves some general (but telling) questions:

- Which assumptions give us the opportunity to live a sane, quality life?
- What must we assume to avoid inconsistencies and contradictions in our thinking?
- When in our history did changing assumptions usher in revolutionary successes?
- Which assumptions let us best explain everything we know we know?

Questions like these allow us to indirectly test our assumptions in ways direct arguments cannot. By asking the right questions, we can trace our knowledge back to its roots. We can examine the assumptions that guide our journey, comparing them with the assumptions of others. In this way, we can discover what sort of assumptions provide the most coherent way to reasonably understand our shared human experience.

The rest of this book takes an indirect approach toward evaluating assumptions. It proves with valid logic the Bible is the best and only explanation for all our knowledge. This book demonstrates one simple truth: *Sound knowledge begins with God's Word.* Reason and revelation are in complete agreement on the matter. To think otherwise is not only unreasonable, but also creates a self-refuting contradiction (what I call the Grand Contradiction).

2

The Right Question

When We Ask The Right Question,
Faith Is More Reasonable Than Doubt

TRUSTING INSTINCTS

Around the turn of the fifth century, Saint Augustine wrote about his amazing conversion experience. He described a moment when he wept uncontrollably. Augustine cried out to God, and suddenly he heard a child's voice say, "Pick up and read." He opened his Bible to a random page and began reading. Then something extraordinary happened. Augustine described it this way: "Instantly, by a light of serenity infused into my heart, all the darkness of doubt vanished away."[1]

Augustine was a reasonable person, numbered among the greatest of Western philosophers. He believed that faith is not a logical conclusion of the human mind. As he saw it, faith starts with a personal religious experience. It could be a marvelous feeling or a subtle urge. But faith is born spontaneously, birthed by a mysterious, involuntary mental event.

How could an intelligent guy like Augustine put so much stock in a personal feeling? Before you answer that question, remember this: We trust all our assumptions the same way. Augustine's account of the origin of his faith is strikingly similar to the way in which we trust our most basic assumptions. We don't trust our senses because we have a good argument. Nor do we rely on our memories after a thorough investigation of all the facts. No. We simply find ourselves with mysterious instincts compelling us to believe things like "What I see is real" and "My memories are accurate history." These intuitions form our assumptions, and our assumptions ground all our knowledge.

Intuitions (religious or otherwise) are beyond our control. But we can still respond to them with suspicion or trust. We can take our instincts at face value, accepting the truths they indicate. Or we can resist their pull and doubt all they tell us about ourselves and our world.

We are free to doubt these basic feelings, but I must give you fair warning. Suspicion here leads to problems. If there's one thing we learn from the history of Western philosophy, it's this: Doubting our basic instincts destroys all hope for knowledge. The Skeptics proved this. They doubted all the intuitions behind their assumptions and, as a result, abandoned their pursuit for knowledge altogether.

Augustine's account of the Christian faith is simple. Faith begins exactly the same way our assumptions do. Feelings beyond our control beckon us to believe. We can accept them at face value. Or we can reject their call for a price.

The price to pay for doubting any basic instinct is to abandon all common sense and force ourselves into some absurd conclusions. In the case of ancient Skeptics, they reasoned they shouldn't reason and made the judgment not to make judgments.

People who ignore their religious intuitions reach their own bizarre conclusions. For example, most atheists say "Humans are just evolved animals," even though they claim to be wiser than animals. They freely decide that freedom is an illusion. They demand justice while insisting, "Morality is a matter of opinion." They promote the thought "Only physical things exist," when their own thoughts clearly aren't physical. Atheists admire beauty, honor love and live by the highest of ideals, but they still insist all this is nothing more than chemical reactions in the brain.

Skeptics who doubt their basic intuitions (religious or otherwise) reach some ridiculous, untenable conclusions. Their lifestyles hardly ever match their theories. And their theories are filled with inconsistencies. They reject all they know deep down is true, and they misunderstand the most meaningful and significant aspects of life.

RELIGIOUS INSTINCTS

My friend started a crazy Christmas tradition. He and his wife browse through thrift stores, looking for the ugliest sweaters they can find. Then, about a week before Christmas, he and a group of his friends go out for dinner, all wearing their awful, ugly sweaters. The sight is hilarious. They definitely draw attention to themselves. They get noticed, whether people enjoy their hijinks or not.

In a way, our religious intuitions are like my poorly dressed friends. Whether we like it or not, religious experiences grab our attention. And in a brief moment they make a lasting impression.

Let's be honest. Now and then we have these religious feelings. Something within us seems to connect us to a deeper spiritual reality. These intuitions can be exhilarating or downright irritating. Sometimes they flood the heart with peace. Other times they prick the conscience with guilt.

These feelings also produce some unusual beliefs. They summon us to believe something greater than ourselves exists (that is, God). They call us to accept some ancient text as the inspired authority on all truth. They even convince us that miracles happen, and that we are unimaginably special. Simply put, religious instincts prompt us to believe in extraordinary things.

Religious experiences aren't ever-present before our minds. And as they fade, we return back to our "normal" lives. But then we are left with a choice. We can either embrace those intuitions and all they stand for. Or we can outright ignore them. We can dismiss their call. And once some time passes, they are forgotten. People might choose to suppress their religious intuitions, but none can deny this fact: Mysterious intuitions occasionally come to the forefront of our minds, calling us to believe.

REASON AND THE HEART

Blaise Pascal was a great French mathematician and inventor. His many contributions to science range from Pascal's Triangle to building the first mechanical calculator. The Pascal programming language was named in his honor. Pascal was one of the greatest intellectuals ever to live. And toward the end of his life, he had a powerful religious experience. After that, his life changed and he devoted his remaining years to writing about the Christian faith.

Pascal used to say there are two ways we know things. The first is by reasoning. The second is by way of the "heart."[2] The former involves scientific study, reviewing evidence, considering arguments and drawing logical conclusions. The latter consists of trusting our basic instincts about truth and reality, taking them at face value and basing all our reasoning on the resulting assumptions.

Clearly, most of our beliefs we call "knowledge" are justified by way of reason. Scientific knowledge about the world comes from studying nature and testing hypotheses. Practical knowledge consists of conclusions drawn from life experiences. Pascal put it this way: "Nature has given us very little knowledge by way of instinct and intuition. All the rest can be known by reasoning."[3]

However, at the same time, we also have a handful of beliefs that don't fit the reasoning mold. Basic assumptions depend solely upon instincts. We can't directly reason about them, nor should we (unless we don't mind reasoning in a circle and committing other logical fallacies). In the words of Pascal, "We know truth, not only by reason, but also by the heart, and it is in this last way that we know first principles."[4]

The fact that we know things in two different ways was a humbling truth for Pascal. He wanted to apply reason to all his beliefs, but he couldn't. Some of our greatest and most meaningful truths aren't known by way of reason. For example, our hearts tell us that life is special, love is honorable and justice is righteous. Our hearts give us meaning and purpose. They reveal beauty, inspire heroes and convict villains. Clearly, our most celebrated truths are known by way of the heart.

As we consider the way we know our greatest truths, one thing becomes apparent. Human reasoning has its limits. And we must react to this fact accordingly. Our logical conclusions deserve the utmost reasonable scrutiny. But we must often trust our hearts' feelings and the assumptions they create apart from any reasoning.

MISDIAGNOSIS

One of my friends experienced a scary ordeal. Without warning he became deathly ill. He visited numerous doctors, but none of them had answers for his illness. As he prepared for the worst, a friend asked him, "Did you get checked for Lyme disease?" A few days later, a new blood test showed that his suspicion was correct. My friend had Lyme disease.

It's hard to believe that one little tick bite caused all those deadly symptoms. How could the experts misdiagnose the disease so easily? My friend's brush with death reminds me of how important it is to properly identify what we are dealing with. Only then can we move forward and solve our problems.

We must assess our beliefs in a way similar to a doctor's diagnosis. Before we embark on our journey to find knowledge, we must first consider our diverse beliefs and decide the best way to understand them. We must know what sort of beliefs we are dealing with before we can discern the proper way to handle their justification.

At the beginning of our pursuit for truth, we have to review all our beliefs and separate the logical conclusions from the assumptions. Once we classify our beliefs in this way, we can get down to the business of reasoning, testing and defending our logical conclusions. But as for our assumptions, they must be accepted by simply trusting our heartfelt intuitions.

This process of classifying our beliefs is essential to any pursuit for knowledge. It is the most important part of our journey. A misdiagnosis of just one belief could derail our search altogether. As the Skeptics of Western philosophy showed us, treating an assumption as your run-of-the-mill conclusion leads to some wonky, untenable theories. But handling a genuine conclusion as an assumption is just as bad. It gives us license to pretty much believe anything we want. For example, children assume that Santa Claus and the Tooth Fairy exist, but most adults rightly treat such tales as testable conclusions demanding our scrutiny.

If we try to justify just one belief in the wrong way, we derail our journey. By misapplying reason, treating assumptions as conclusions and vice versa, we destroy everything reason can offer. Therefore, when we encounter a logical conclusion, we should prove its worth through critical reasoning. But when it's time to assume, we must hold reason in check and listen to our heart's intuitions. Otherwise, we demand too much from a genuine assumption and not enough from a logical conclusion, thereby putting our entire search for knowledge in jeopardy.

RELIGIOUS BELIEFS

Usually it's pretty easy to separate conclusions from assumptions. Truths like "Water freezes at 0 degrees Celsius" and "Abraham Lincoln was the sixteenth U.S. president" are the sort of beliefs we know through science, history and general observations. Beliefs like these are clearly logical conclusions.

Other beliefs are obviously assumptions. We don't trust our senses as a result of a good argument. We don't believe our memories are correct through debate. No. Deep down within our hearts we feel we can trust our senses and our memories. Beliefs like these are not the product of human will. Nor do they result from reasoning. Our assumptions might be few in number compared with our logical conclusions. But this doesn't do away with the fact that we must "know" some powerful truths by way of the heart's intuitions. Nor should it automatically count against the reasonableness of the beliefs we must assume as our greatest truths.

This distinction between a "conclusion" and an "assumption" is simple enough. But as we move along the path to truth, we stumble onto some very peculiar beliefs. Religious beliefs like "God exists" and "An ancient, sacred text is true" stand out as special beliefs unique to all others. They are as mysterious as they are profound. They hold the greatest significance for believers and evoke the mightiest contempt from nonreligious people.

What do we do with these religious beliefs? How should we go about understanding them? And how do they fit into our search for knowledge?

Should we treat our religious beliefs as logical conclusions? Or should we trust them as we do our assumptions?

Nothing from the human experience clearly indicates how we should classify religious beliefs. And we can't just assume that all religious beliefs are logical conclusions without a good reason. Nor should we arbitrarily suppose they are assumptions. In both cases, we would have a logical fallacy on our hands.

We need good reasons to support the way we go about justifying religious beliefs. But we can't directly argue for either position. Admittedly, having no argument is completely unreasonable. But offering a direct argument would depend upon many unexamined assumptions, thereby heaping circular reasoning on top of our dilemma.

The challenge is evident. Mystery shrouds our religious beliefs. They are so extraordinary it makes them difficult to classify with any confidence. And when we directly reason about them, we run into a host of logical fallacies. Nonetheless, we must still try to find some logical way to address the above question. It is imperative for us to reasonably determine the nature of a religious belief, whether it is rightly called an assumption or a logical conclusion, before we can progress in our journey for knowledge.

COMPARE AND CONTRAST

When I was a second-grade teacher, I taught my students a simple strategy for learning. I drew a Venn diagram on the board and gave them the assignment of comparing two *Star Wars* characters: Luke Skywalker and Darth Vader.

The students drew their own overlapping circles. Within each circle, they wrote down all the similar qualities Luke and Vader shared. Outside the circles, they listed all their differences. Through a simple comparison like this, they learned a great deal about these two characters.

I suggest we use the same kind of scientific study to understand the nature of religious beliefs. By comparing and contrasting all our different beliefs, we gain great insight into the best way to pursue truth. A simple comparison is the most objective way to understand where religion fits into our search for knowledge. This review offers us insight into the most reasonable way to handle the justification of our religious beliefs.

Religious beliefs are as peculiar as they are mysterious, so it's initially unclear how we should handle their justification. Therefore, we must compare our religious beliefs to our "better-known" beliefs. If religious beliefs exhibit qualities similar to our standard logical conclusions, then it's reasonable to treat the justification of Christian faith as we would justify a testable scientific hypothesis. On the other hand, if religious beliefs display characteristics commonly found in our assumptions, it's most reasonable to treat their justification in a like manner. In sum, we must ask ourselves "Do religious beliefs have more in common with our logical conclusions or our basic assumptions?" The answer to this question will determine the most logical approach to take for justifying any religious belief, including faith in Jesus Christ.

A comparative study is a must, a prerequisite for any debate over the reasonableness of religion. It is the most scientific way to see how religion should fit into our pursuit for knowledge. It is also the best way to avoid all the circular reasoning behind debates over God's existence. Consider this: The moment anyone starts arguing against (or for) Christian faith, they have already assumed faith is something we can (and should) argue about.

But have debaters proven this assumption is most reasonable? No. They naively assert "Faith is just another conclusion of human logic," but offer no good reason to think such a thing. And how could they? If participants of the God debate tried to argue for their position, they would only reason in a circle about it. In this way, assumptions about the nature of our religious beliefs are just like any other assumption. And no one can directly prove with sound reasoning that an assumption is true.

So, let's set aside all our opinions about religion. Let's put away all our biases and traditions. Let's dispense with the vicious circular reasoning. Now, ask this straightforward question: How should we understand the justification of a religious belief? A simple comparison and contrast of all our beliefs gives us the most reasonable answer to this question.

On one hand, we have our logical conclusions. On the other hand, we have our assumptions. Consider the characteristics of our logical, scientific conclusions:

- Conclusions are always about physical objects.
- Conclusions always deal with natural causes and effects.
- Conclusions depend upon empirical studies and laboratory tests.
- Conclusions offer verifiable predictions about the natural world.
- Conclusions are based on deliberate, intentional decisions.
- Conclusions are the product of discursive reasoning.
- Conclusions are known by weighing probabilities.
- Conclusions represent specific, concrete instances of knowledge.
- Conclusions result at the end of the reasoning process.

Now, contrast these traits with the qualities exhibited by our common assumptions:

- Assumptions are not always about physical objects.
- Assumptions do not always deal with natural causes and effects.
- Assumptions do not depend upon empirical studies and laboratory tests.
- Assumptions do not always offer verifiable predictions about the natural world.
- Assumptions are based on involuntary, uncontrollable feelings.
- Assumptions are the product of immediate intuitions.
- Assumptions are known with relative certainty.
- Assumptions create a general context for beliefs, thereby making knowledge possible.
- Assumptions both begin and guide the reasoning process.

Notice the stark differences between these two kinds of beliefs. It is one thing to say, "Water freezes at 0 degrees Celsius," and quite another to say, "We have the freedom to live moral lives." The former is a conclusion about the concrete physics of our natural world. The latter is a belief about an abstract element of our reality.

Now, here is the question at hand: Do religious beliefs most closely resemble a logical conclusion or an assumption? Which of these two kinds of familiar beliefs have the most in common with our unusual religious beliefs?

Surely, a religious belief like "God exists" is not about a physical object. An eternal God does not come from a natural cause. And we can't take a biopsy of God for laboratory testing. Nor can we consistently predict the behavior of our natural world from theology.

Furthermore, most religious people admit that faith is an immediate reaction to an involuntary spiritual experience. This sort of faith is not based on reasonable tests. Nevertheless, faith is a certainty in the minds of believers. Finally, religion shades the perspective of a believer, effectively creating a worldview that determines how he or she will interpret the human experience.

Therefore, from a simple comparison and contrast of all our beliefs, one thing is clear. By all rational accounts, religious beliefs share a substantial number of characteristics with assumptions. Furthermore, religious beliefs have absolutely nothing in common with logical conclusions. Given these indisputable facts, a case is easily made for treating the justification of religious beliefs as we do our other assumptions about truth and reality. This logic applies to the justification of Christian faith as well. Moreover, the way of arguments and the scientific method are obviously inappropriate for directly justifying a religious belief.

Based on a simple comparison of our beliefs and an argument from analogy, it is most reasonable to take our religious intuitions at face value, trusting them as we would any other instinct that grounds a better-known assumption. Assumptions are justified by compelling instincts. Doubting such feelings destroys any hope for sound knowledge. This situation regarding assumptions applies to our religious beliefs as well. And objective, noncircular reasoning leads us to that conclusion every time.

DO ALL PEOPLE HAVE RELIGIOUS FEELINGS?

You might be surprised to hear some people claim they've never experienced a religious intuition. I can't reasonably speak about another person's internal feelings. What I can say is "It's never too late." Anyone at any time can have a personal religious encounter. As long as people are open-minded and seeking truth, a religious experience is always possible.

Regardless, even if someone never has a religious experience, that still doesn't count against the logic of this argument. Suppose for a moment that religious experiences aren't universal (that is, religious intuitions aren't experienced by everyone). This wouldn't necessarily make them irrational or untrue.

An atheist's objection along these lines is based on nothing more than circular reasoning. He or she begins reasoning with the assumptions "Truth is uniformly accessed" and "Truth is universally experienced." After first assuming these things, an atheist then concludes "Religious experiences aren't legit because they aren't always the same (uniformly accessed) and they aren't experienced by all (universally experienced)." But this conclusion is the very thing the atheist first assumed!

Even worse, these secular assumptions in question contradict their own message. Are these assumptions held by everyone (are they universal)? Are they reached the same way by all people (are they uniformly accessed)? No. These assumptions don't even meet their own demands. They don't pass their own truth standards!

Therefore, any objection against the reasonableness of faith based on some people not having religious experiences is both circular and self-defeating. In the end, we have no good reason to think trusting religious experiences as we do our assumptions is necessarily unreasonable.

DEBATING RELIGIOUS BELIEFS

The 2016 U.S. presidential race was a strange moment in American politics. The leading candidates included a politician under FBI investigation and a billionaire businessman-reality TV star. Only one thing was normal about the race: America's choice for president was a matter of the candidate people disliked the least. Such is politics.

Early in his campaign, Republican candidate Marco Rubio showed great promise. But something odd happened in one of his debates. When asked a variety of questions, Rubio responded with the same scripted line over and over again. After repeating himself four times, it seemed like he wasn't even listening to the moderators. And when the New Hampshire debate ended, all the buzz was about Rubio's poor performance. A month later Marco Rubio suspended his campaign.

Rubio's debate performance in early 2016 is a great example of how public debates are seldom about the search for truth. More often than not, debaters just want to prove a point. It's often this way in politics, as it is in religious debates.

The debate over God's existence has raged for over two millennia. Arguments about a First Cause and a Designer are pitted against the Problem of Evil and other proofs. But after two thousand years of arguing, no one is the wiser. The age-old God debate is still inconclusive. Discourse has failed to reveal the truth. Could it be this is because we are asking the wrong questions?

Debaters often assume without question that we should treat the justification of religious beliefs as we do our common logical conclusions. The entire God debate hinges on this assumption. But why should we believe this? In all the arguing, no one ever gives a good reason for the debate's greatest assumption (the assumption that faith in God is a logical conclusion). As people reason about faith, they fail to ask the most important question: "How should we go about justifying religious beliefs?" Because of this shocking oversight, the old God debate gets us no closer to the truth.

The traditional God debate is little more than a distraction (a red herring fallacy as the philosophers call it), keeping us from the real issue at hand. Most participants are just out to prove their point. And all participants naively assume without good reason that religious beliefs are logical conclusions, voluntary decisions made by the human will. All the while, debaters fail to ask, and answer, the question of how to understand the justification of our religious beliefs.

Before the God debate can have any meaning to us, we must determine the most reasonable way to justify our religious beliefs. If we have good reason to think our religious beliefs should be treated as assumptions, then the classical debate has no significance whatsoever. And since our comparison of beliefs in this chapter yields a powerful argument from analogy (proving it's most reasonable to treat faith in God like we would any other assumption about truth and reality) the traditional God debate is now dead. So long as the God debate is based on a faulty, unexamined assumption, all its arguments have no meaning for us.

Arguments are only as good as their assumptions. Interpretations of the evidence are guided by one's assumptions. If a debater's assumptions are bad, what does that say about his or her arguments? How can we take any argument seriously if it's based on an unreasonable assumption?

THE RIGHT QUESTION

Have you ever had a challenging job interview? A man or woman in a suit grills you with questions. He or she silently jots down your responses. And near the end of the inquisition, the prospective employer surprisingly asks you, "Do you have any questions for me?" When this happens to me, I think, "*Who's doing the interviewing here?*"

There's a reason why employers turn the interview around and let the potential employee ask questions. The questions we ask are just as telling as our answers. Robert Half, an employment recruiting group, has a saying: Asking the right questions is just as important as giving the right answers. This is true in our pursuit for knowledge as well.

The great philosopher Bertrand Russell once said, "In all affairs, it's a healthy thing now and then to hang a question mark on the things you have long taken for granted."[5] He was absolutely right. We must review our assumptions now and then to ensure that our quest for truth is still on course. We must consider our unexamined beliefs to determine if we are headed in the right direction. And we must ask the right questions to get to the truth.

But sometimes no one is asking the right questions. The God debate is an excellent example. Participants gather their evidence, piece together their arguments and rehearse their talking points. But they all fail to realize that assumptions drive the debate. One debater assumes a god might exist, a god might be known and religious experiences are trustworthy, while the other debater doesn't.

How can two intelligent people review the same body of evidence and arrive at vastly different conclusions? The reason is not found in the arguments. The actual disagreement has to do with their assumptions about truth and reality. The real question to debate is "Should we treat a religious belief as a logical conclusion or as an assumption?" And because religious beliefs so closely resemble our assumptions, the most reasonable answer to this question is "Faith in God is not the sort of thing we can directly argue about."

THE DEATH OF THE GOD DEBATE

On April 8, 1966, *TIME* magazine shocked the world when it published an issue with a black cover and the title in bold red letters: "Is God Dead?" The cover story was about the Western world's gradual shift away from orthodox Christianity and toward a secular society. In the 1960s this trend in America was often referred to as "the Death of God" movement.

It's silly to suggest that God actually lives or dies because of what we think. *TIME*'s controversial article was really about the relevance of God in our lives. Many people now turn to secular science and philosophy as their ultimate source for truth. For nonreligious people, faith has no part in their pursuit for knowledge. For these people, religion appears unreasonable. But nothing could be further from the truth.

If only we ask the right questions, we discover it's most reasonable to trust our religious intuitions just like we trust our other basic instincts. If we have the courage to follow reason wherever it leads, we find that Christian faith is much more reasonable than doubt.

For all intents and purposes, it is the whole classical God debate that has died. The old way of apologetics has ended. Arguments about a First Cause, a Designer, problems with evil, etc. have no more meaning for our journey. As long as people fail to ask the right questions and neglect the real issues surrounding their assumptions, we make no progress toward truth. And only the indirect evaluation outlined in this book can soundly show us the best assumptions to make sense of our shared human experience.

But have no fear. From the death of the old debate, reasonable faith is born. And this is to everyone's benefit, because it is the only way to achieve sound knowledge. Christians should be encouraged by this demise, for reasoning guided by the right questions shows us that faith is entirely reasonable. But nonreligious people should be concerned because their conclusions (which might appear reasonable on the surface) are based on a number of problematic assumptions. Not the least of which is the extremely irrational assumption that we should treat unusual religious beliefs as if they are common logical conclusions.

3

The Grand Contradiction

Bad Assumptions Lead To A Self-Refuting Contradiction

A BAD FOUNDATION

The Lotus Riverside is an apartment complex in the suburban Minhang district of Shanghai, China. Its claim to fame is an unfortunate event. During construction in 2009, one of the complex's thirteen-story buildings collapsed. Authorities investigated the scene and discovered the new thirty-eight million-dollar building toppled because it was constructed on a bad foundation.[1]

The *South China Morning Post* reported that its builder used faulty concrete pilings.[2] The Lotus Riverside Block 7 looked like a magnificent apartment building on the surface. However, its foundation was flawed. And as the world discovered, a building is only as stable as its foundation.

The Lotus Riverside debacle is an excellent example of how important it is to begin with a good foundation. Our need for a firm foundation applies not only to the construction industry. A good foundation is especially important to our pursuit for knowledge.

Assumptions are the foundation of knowledge. All our reasoning rests upon them. We must start reasoning with the best assumptions; otherwise, we build knowledge on shaky ground. And bad assumptions lead to flawed conclusions. Therefore, it is essential for us to examine the foundation of our knowledge to discover the surest footing for reason.

In chapter two we looked at an argument based on experience (an *a posteriori* argument as the philosophers call it). From a scientific comparison of all our beliefs, we discovered religious beliefs most closely resemble our other better-known assumptions. In fact, we learned that religious beliefs have absolutely nothing in common with logical conclusions. Therefore, by arguing from analogy, it's most reasonable to treat the justification of Christian faith in the same manner we justify other assumptions. Furthermore, it would be quite irrational to handle the justification of any religious belief as we would a scientific hypothesis.

Here in chapter three, we consider an *a priori* argument (that is, an argument not based on experience, but solely on reason). This involves taking a look at the very idea of "knowledge" and what it means for knowledge to be sound. From this sort of proof, one thing is evident: Sound knowledge is impossible on secular assumptions. The secular agenda for knowledge leads people into a great contradiction.

The secular agenda for knowledge is a general plan to understand the world without reference to the supernatural. Followers of this agenda dismiss religion from all rational conversations. Under the guise of reason, they try to brand religious beliefs as ignorant, useless superstitions. They give no place to God in their search for knowledge, believing that knowledge is only about physical things we can see and touch. They reject the Bible, looking to human reason as the sole basis for knowledge. Atheists, agnostics, naturalists, materialists and most humanists promote this secular agenda. These people believe supernatural things either don't exist or aren't important. And just like the Lotus Riverside Block 7, the secular agenda has a problem with its foundation.

PROTAGORAS'S PRINCIPLE

Protagoras was the original professional philosopher of ancient Greece. He was the first full-time Sophist (which was a teacher for hire in the ancient world). Little is known about this mysterious man. What we do know is Protagoras introduced the premiere secular assumption to Western philosophy. Since the beginning, his principle "Man is the measure of all things" has grounded Western philosophy and science.[3]

It isn't clear exactly what Protagoras meant when he proclaimed, "Man is the measure of all things." But in simple terms, his assumption implies that knowledge begins and ends with human reasoning. According to him, reason deals with human thoughts about our natural world. Knowledge is about things we can see and touch. And he assumed people have the final say on what knowledge is and how to go about getting it.

If we make this sort of humanistic assumption, where does religion fit into our journey? If human reason is the final authority on all truth, what does that mean for God's Word, the Bible? Protagoras called people to judge religious beliefs just like they would a logical conclusion. He expected us to run our scientific tests, form our arguments and draw our logical conclusions as if we are the final judge on religious matters.

Initially, being the judge of all things doesn't sound bad. It actually feels empowering, even liberating. But does this premiere assumption of Western philosophy allow us to reason in the best possible way? Is there a good reason to think Protagoras's principle is correct?

"TYING DOWN" OUR BELIEFS

Greek mythology describes Daedalus as the greatest craftsman who ever lived. He built an elaborate labyrinth to imprison the Minotaur. He also made himself wings that let him fly like the gods. He was the most famous artist and inventor of his day.

Plato mentioned Daedalus when describing how we know things. During a conversation with Meno, Socrates explained that our beliefs must be tied down like Daedalus's beautiful statues. Apparently, these statues were so precious the owners locked them with chains to prevent theft. Plato taught that we must do the same with our beliefs, tying them down with our arguments and evidence to keep them from aimlessly wandering away.[4]

Plato's account touches on what I call our Natural Need for Evidence. It's natural for us to seek arguments and evidence to support our beliefs. It's necessary for us to judge and test our logical conclusions. Only after we tie down our beliefs with supporting proofs can we say we have knowledge. In the words of the philosophers, "We must justify our beliefs with good reasons."

Most philosophers define knowledge as a belief that is both true and justified. If a belief is not supported by arguments and evidence, then it's nothing more than a mere opinion. Opinions may or may not be true. And if an opinion happens to be true, it's simply a lucky guess. But knowledge is much more than an opinion or a lucky guess. To know something means to have a true belief that is justified in a reasonable way.

INFINITE REGRESS

Have you ever stood between two mirrors? They create an optical illusion that looks like an infinite chain of reflections. The images seem to get smaller and smaller until finally reaching a vanishing point. This illusion is called an "infinite regress." The images appear to go on without end.

In our pursuit for truth, something interesting happens when we pair Protagoras's principle with our Natural Need for Evidence. If our foundation for knowledge contains the assumption "Man is the measure of all things" along with the assumption "We must support our beliefs with good reasons," a problem immediately develops:

1. We must justify all our beliefs with good reasons.
2. We must rely solely on human reasoning to justify beliefs.
3. However, we can't justify our most important beliefs, our assumptions about truth and reality, with human reasoning.

When we pair Plato's Natural Need for Evidence (premise 1) with Protagoras's secular assumption (premise 2), we make it impossible to begin reasoning! How so? We must make some assumptions about what knowledge is before we can seek it. We have to decide what is real and true before we can get down to the business of reasoning. We have to make some assumptions.

But human reasoning can't offer us a good reason for our assumptions. At best, we can only offer circular reasons (which aren't good reasons). If we're consistent, taking our proven rules of reasoning seriously, then our assumptions aren't justified. Consequently, we shouldn't think they are true. And since we can't trust our assumptions, we can't take the very first step of our journey toward truth. Suddenly, we are paralyzed by our humanity. And knowledge is impossible!

What if we refuse to accept this roadblock? What if we insist on secular assumptions but try to avoid the circular reasoning? What happens if we go ahead and try to justify an assumption with secular reasoning? We get caught up in an infinite regress of arguments.

Every argument is based on a number of assumptions. When we offer an argument to justify one of our assumptions, we must ask, "What assumptions is this argument based on?" Now we have a second group of assumptions to justify. Let's put together a second argument to justify the assumptions of the first argument. Again, the second argument brings its own assumptions to the exercise. At this point, we need a third argument (along with its assumptions) to justify the second argument's assumptions. To make a long story short, the moment we try to directly justify any assumption, we suddenly have on our hands an infinite regress of arguments with no end in sight.

If we are serious about the Natural Need for Evidence, then we must justify all our beliefs with good reasons. But when man is the measure of all things, we cannot justify our foundational beliefs (our most basic assumptions) about what is real and true. If we try, we trap ourselves in an infinite regress similar to our image of standing between two mirrors. How can we ever begin reasoning the way both Protagoras and Plato described?

A FREE PASS

While I was growing up, I played Monopoly with my friends. My goal was to buy all the properties I could and quickly build hotels on them. If I was having a good game, I eventually owned an entire corner of the board. Then it was impossible to pass through my neighborhood without paying me rent.

My opponents would beg me to give them a "free pass" through my domain. Sometimes I would let them land on my property rent-free. Other times I would force them into bankruptcy. It didn't seem fair to give some opponents a free pass while demanding payment from others. But at the time, I wasn't too concerned about that. I just wanted to win.

Secular philosophers remind me of how I played Monopoly. At the foundation of their knowledge, philosophers have paired two assumptions that don't mix. They cling to Protagoras's principle, claiming "Man is the measure of all things." They also insist "We need good reasons to count a belief as knowledge," as Plato assumed. From the get-go, they have trapped themselves between two mirrors, unable to begin reasoning. The only way for them to start reasoning is to arbitrarily give some of their assumptions a free pass and say, "We don't need to justify our assumptions with good arguments."

This dilemma facing secular philosophers is nothing new. Ancient Skeptics wrestled with this problem to great lengths. Their conclusion: Give up the pursuit for knowledge and suspend judgment. They made a decision to not make decisions. In the end, the Skeptics didn't offer a real solution.

Other secular philosophers and scientists fared no better. They assumed knowledge is possible. But they simply gave their favorite assumptions a free pass. They just accepted their assumptions as true without a good reason. They suspended their best practices long enough to assume what they wanted to assume. Ultimately, they abandoned scrutiny at the most important moment of their journey. And since when has forgoing arguments and evidence led to truth?

My Monopoly opponents called such inconsistencies a double standard. The Oxford Dictionary defines a double standard as "A rule or principle that is unfairly applied in different ways."[5] When you have useful, proven rules of logic and decide now and then to ignore them for the sake of expediency (or some other ulterior motive), most people call this discrimination. This sort of hypocrisy is more about playing favorites than seeking truth.

Even worse, when people give their assumptions a free pass, they commit a number of logical fallacies. They are essentially saying, "My assumptions lead me to the kind of knowledge I think best," or "I feel like my assumptions are true." These examples are nothing more than what the philosophers call an *argumentum ad consequentiam* (an argument to the consequences) or an *argumentum ad passiones* (an argument to the emotions). Clearly, logical fallacies like these are not a sound path to knowledge either.

To begin reasoning, we can't simply hand out free passes to our favorite assumptions! This is not just arbitrary and inconsistent; it is hypocritical and entirely illogical.

THE LAW OF NONCONTRADICTION

Have you ever read a *Garfield* comic strip? The witty cat always has something funny to say. My favorite picture of Garfield shows him sitting at a table with a cup of coffee in his hand. Wearing pajamas and sporting drowsy eyes, Garfield comments, "Good morning is a contradiction of terms." I can relate to Garfield. I'm definitely not a morning person.

In this comic strip Garfield reminds me of a philosopher. The greatest rule of reason to come out of Western philosophy is the law of noncontradiction. Since the time of Aristotle, the rule has been a standard litmus test for all that is true and real. The law simply states, "Nothing can be both A and not A at the same time." A solid-colored ball cannot be both red and blue at the same time. A person can't be happy and sad in the same moment.

This proven rule of reason guides all common sense. It helps us understand the natural world. Philosophers depend upon the law of noncontradiction as their greatest tool to test all beliefs. Everyone uses the law to distinguish truth from falsehood.

If one of our beliefs contradicts another, we must investigate them thoroughly. Reason demands we reject any belief (even an assumption) if it causes a contradiction with the majority of our other beliefs. And if any idea of the human mind contains a contradiction, we must set it aside as bad. This law is so essential to our pursuit for knowledge that Ludwig Wittgenstein once said, "It is the business of philosophy to understand our contradictions."[6] In short, if any person contradicts himself or herself, that person does not possess truth.

THE GRAND CONTRADICTION

When philosophers and scientists begin their search for truth with secular assumptions, pairing Protagoras's principle with Plato's Natural Need for Evidence, they run into what I call "the Grand Contradiction." These people reject God's Word, the Bible, as the absolute authority on truth. They replace God's revealed truths with human assumptions and other man-made principles. Consequently, they begin reasoning with many contradictions.

Imposing the secular agenda on knowledge is like that building in China we learned about at the beginning of this chapter. On the surface, secular reasoning appears reasonable. But deep down at its foundation, a nonreligious person's reasoning is based on nothing more than inconsistencies and contradictions. Even the most brilliant of atheists and agnostics contradict themselves in order to begin reasoning. They break the very rules of logic they say we must always follow.

The moment people begin reasoning solely by their rational faculties and of their own accord, they break these fundamental principles of good reasoning:

- Sound knowledge depends on consistent reasoning.
- Sound knowledge requires supporting arguments and proofs.
- Sound knowledge is reached through noncircular reasoning.
- Sound knowledge involves engaging and resolving our problems.
- Sound knowledge is objective.
- Sound knowledge is always without contradiction.

First, nonreligious people must reason inconsistently just to begin reasoning. Philosophers tell us we should be critical, questioning all of our beliefs. At the risk of being biased or careless, we should consistently scrutinize all our beliefs. Clearly, consistency is a hallmark of good reasoning.

But proponents of the secular agenda begin reasoning with a great inconsistency. They momentarily set aside scrutiny to make a number of assumptions about what is real and true. They forgo the demands of reason to begin reasoning. Their human assumptions are fashioned in an unacceptable manner, inconsistent with Western philosophy's norms for good reasoning. And when they give their assumptions a free pass, their inconsistency becomes obvious.

Second, secular philosophers ignore the Natural Need for Evidence to reason about evidence. As W. K. Clifford once said, "It is wrong always, everywhere and for anyone, to believe anything upon insufficient evidence."[7] Good supporting arguments are a must for us to count any belief as knowledge.

But people beholden to a secular agenda for knowledge are incapable of giving good arguments for their assumptions. If they try to directly justify a human assumption, they find themselves trapped in an infinite regress of arguments. The only other option they have is to abandon their evidentiary standards at the moment they need them most.

Third, nonreligious people begin with circular reasoning to establish their proven rule against circular reasoning. Aristotle maintained, "A circular demonstration is no demonstration at all."[8] If people are allowed to reason in a circle, they can pretty much prove anything. Obviously, circular reasoning does not lead to knowledge.

But this is precisely what secular philosophers and scientists do when they consider the correctness of their assumptions. Arguments for any human assumption depend upon the very assumption in question. As proponents of the secular agenda reflect on their basic assumptions, they essentially create a foundation for knowledge swirling with circular thought.

Fourth, secular scientists ignore all these problems to solve other problems. Common sense tells us that ignoring some of our problems to retain a comfortable, familiar view of the world is no way to real knowledge.

Subscribers to the secular agenda fail to attend to their greatest problems. Secular scientists thoroughly engage in problem-solving study of our natural world. But lurking deep down within the foundation of their thinking, huge philosophical problems are left unresolved.

Fifth, secular philosophers base their reasoning on feelings in order to prohibit reason's dependence on feelings. Reason tells us time and time again that decisions based exclusively on our natural feelings aren't dependable. A conclusion based on emotional feelings is a logical fallacy the philosophers call an emotional appeal.

But secular philosophers and scientists base their assumptions on nothing more than feelings. Assumptions form out of mysterious feelings, which are quite personal and subjective. Secular philosophers and scientists begin their pursuit for knowledge with the very sort of feelings they consider suspect.

Sixth, proponents of a secular agenda for knowledge contradict themselves to establish the law of noncontradiction. The law of noncontradiction is one of our most valuable tools for understanding the world. Its dependability has been proven time and time again. Western philosophy and science have consistently relied upon this rule for reasoning since the days of Aristotle.

But nonreligious people contradict themselves the moment they begin reasoning. Secular philosophers say, "We must reason consistently," but they inconsistently give their initial assumptions about truth and reality a free pass. They demand, "Everyone must have good reasons for their beliefs," but they have none to offer for their most important beliefs. They claim, "Circular reasoning is unacceptable," but they reason in a circle when they directly argue for their assumptions. Secular scientists call us to examine all our problems, but they neglect their own problems with the foundation of their knowledge. Secular philosophers say, "Knowledge is not based on subjective feelings," but secular assumptions always emerge from subjective feelings.

In sum, secular philosophers and scientists proclaim, "The law of noncontradiction is a litmus test for all that is reasonable," but the way they begin reasoning blatantly contradicts everything they claim is reasonable. People intent on rejecting God's Word break their own rules for reasoning as they begin reasoning. To uphold the law of noncontradiction, they must initially contradict themselves. This is the Grand Contradiction, the byproduct of a secular agenda for knowledge. It is the faulty foundation upon which all secular reasoning rests.

SELF-REFUTING POSITIONS

In the 1960s, a novel titled *Catch-22* was published. Set during World War II, the story followed the life of a bombardier named John Yossarian. Conditions for the servicemen were so perilous that they tried to figure out ways to get discharged. But with the military's absurd policy for release, it was impossible to escape.

Here was Yossarian's dilemma: If an airman was mentally unfit to fly, he could be released. But the act of applying for release (a rational behavior) demonstrated sanity. Thus, the airmen were caught in a "catch-22." If they tried to petition for release, they provided the government with evidence against the very thing they hoped to achieve.

This catch-22 situation is an excellent example of a "self-refuting" position. The airmen desperately wanted a discharge. But in building a case for their release (a case based on them being mentally unfit), they were ultimately creating a case against their release (because the act of petitioning for release proved they were mentally fit). Any movement toward escape would be self-defeating, ultimately ensuring failure.

Proponents of the secular agenda for knowledge put themselves in a catch-22 when they begin reasoning with secular assumptions. They create a self-refuting kind of knowledge. The moment people adopt a secular agenda, pairing Protagoras's assumption with our Natural Need for Evidence, they destroy the possibility for sound knowledge (that is, knowledge free from contradictions).

They make sound knowledge impossible because they insist on a godless, nonreligious picture of the world. By reasoning without God's guidance, they commit the Grand Contradiction. In this way, all who adopt the secular agenda for knowledge undermine their search for truth. The more people reason without God's Word, the more they contradict themselves. And contradictions are clearly not the path to knowledge.

A BAD PAIRING

One morning I thought it would be a great idea to surprise my family by making French toast for breakfast. I always add vanilla extract to the batter as my secret ingredient. My wife loves my French toast, but on that fateful morning she cringed when she tasted her first bite. After examining all my ingredients, I discovered the problem. The vanilla bottle looked exactly like a bottle of cough syrup. My secret ingredient that morning was Children's Dimetapp!

Some things just don't go well together. Regarding the foundation of knowledge, two assumptions don't mix. Plato's assumption says we must have supporting arguments for all our human beliefs. Protagoras's assumption asserts that human beliefs are all we have to work with, thereby making men and women the final judges on all matters. When these two assumptions come together in a foundation, the Grand Contradiction results.

A bad pairing of assumptions creates this impossible situation. But why are most philosophers and scientists so optimistic about the secular agenda for knowledge? Some explain their Grand Contradiction away with logical fallacies. Others outright ignore the problem. The only way to justify their secular assumptions is to use bad reasoning or no reasoning at all. Neither option is the way to sound knowledge.

History shows us that Western philosophy has been driven by the assumptions of Protagoras and Plato. But sound logic proves these two assumptions lead to an untenable situation. Reason demands one thing: We must consider the pairing of these two incompatible assumptions and revise (or even reject) the assumption that proves itself least reasonable. This is the only way to avoid the Grand Contradiction and attain sound knowledge.

On one hand, we have Plato's Natural Need for Evidence. It's a proven principle, universally accepted by all reasonable people. By definition, reasoning necessarily involves evidentiary reviews. Even those who dare argue against the need for evidence only prove the principle's worth (by the very fact they are still arguing). It's easy to see that our Natural Need for Evidence is a necessary part of all reasoning.

On the other hand, we have Protagoras's assumption, "Man is the measure of all things."[9] This is a belief much more controversial and less essential for reasoning. A recent study by Pew Research shows that over half of the world's population believe in a god (not a man) as the ultimate bearer of truth and the absolute measure of all things.[10] Furthermore, many philosophers and scientists believe in a god whose knowledge is superior to ours. These facts prove that Protagoras's secular assumption is not necessary for reasoning. Therefore, Protagoras's principle is much more expendable than Plato's Natural Need for Evidence.

So, which of these two assumptions seems more suspect? Clearly Protagoras's principle is easier to doubt than our Natural Need for Evidence. If we must reject one of the two assumptions, then let us do away with Protagoras's principle. Even if we wanted to, we could never throw away the Natural Need for Evidence. The practice of supporting our beliefs with good arguments and evidence is necessary for reason to be reason. Therefore, to resolve the Grand Contradiction and create a coherent body of beliefs we must get rid of the premiere secular assumption traditionally guiding Western philosophy and science. We must toss out Protagoras's assumption "Man is the measure of all things." Only then is sound knowledge (that is, knowledge free from contradictions) possible. And in the next chapter you will discover exactly how abandoning the secular agenda opens the door to sound knowledge.

SOUND KNOWLEDGE

A summary of this chapter yields the following argument:

1. Sound knowledge is knowledge without contradictions.
2. Those who endorse a secular agenda begin their search for knowledge with a contradiction (the Grand Contradiction).
3. Therefore, sound knowledge is impossible for any follower of a secular agenda.

The Grand Contradiction tells us that sound knowledge is impossible the moment someone begins reasoning with secular assumptions. Logic demands we get rid of any assumption causing this contradiction. And a simple review of our greatest assumptions reveals that Protagoras's principle must go, for we could never deny our Natural Need for Evidence.

Now, you might wonder, "Do we have sound knowledge in the first place?" If sound knowledge doesn't exist, then the argument fails. Perhaps self-contradictions are just an unavoidable part of life?

It's easy to say that we don't have sound knowledge, but history proves otherwise. When we consider the amazing achievements of Western science, we must admit that we do have sound knowledge. Through science, we gain a great deal of knowledge about the physical world. If anything counts as sound knowledge, it's what we know from modern science. But the idea that modern science was born out of circular reasoning and contradictions seems absurd, even impossible.

As a follow-up, you might also wonder, "Do nonreligious people have any knowledge at all?" It would be silly to think secular scientists don't know something. The Grand Contradiction doesn't imply that atheists and naturalists are utterly ignorant. Rather, it indicates that something has gone awry in their thinking. A misstep, a mistaken assumption, keeps nonreligious people from logically explaining all their knowledge.

Case in point: The method secular scientists use to pursue knowledge is not entirely consistent. Nor is their knowledge comprehensive in its scope. Their reasoning isn't consistent because they overlook their assumptions, giving them a most unscientific free pass. And their knowledge isn't comprehensive either, because science cannot address paramount questions about the truthfulness of its own assumptions. The brilliant Kurt Gödel mathematically proved this by way of his Incompleteness Theorems.

Moreover, modern science can't even answer our most meaningful questions. Who are we? Why are we here? How should we live? Science gives us useful knowledge about the physical world, but it can't intelligibly speak about the broader context of our human experience. It explains the "how" of nature, but neglects the "why" behind it all.

At best, secular science yields only a shortsighted, myopic picture of reality. When scientists try to overreach, venturing from physics into metaphysics, they come up with some bizarre conclusions: An orderly universe came from random disorder, life rose out of lifeless happenstance, humans are just evolved animals, the mind is only physical, the will is not free, love is merely chemical reactions in the brain, morality is a matter of opinions, and so on. And all the while, speculations like these are never verified by actual observations.

Don't get me wrong. Science has a wonderful place in our search for truth. And secular scientists clearly have knowledge. But what kind of knowledge do secular assumptions yield? A nonreligious person's search for truth always begins with the Grand Contradiction and ends with fragments of truth mingled with some illogical speculations. His or her reasoning is filled with inconsistencies, yielding a big picture of reality that's always skewed. Proponents of the secular agenda might have knowledge in some respect, but it's surely not "sound knowledge" (knowledge free from inconsistency and contradiction). And the fact that proponents of the secular agenda begin with the Grand Contradiction is most revealing, because reason tells us that contradictions are not the way to truth.

4

A Special Revelation

Supernatural Faith In A Special Revelation
Is The Only Basis For Sound Knowledge

SOLVING PROBLEMS

One of the greatest problem solvers to ever live was a high school dropout named Albert Einstein. Upon the rise of Nazi Germany, young Einstein fled his homeland. He reached Switzerland and applied to a new school. Despite failing most of his entrance exam, his exceptional skills in mathematics and physics earned him an acceptance letter.

After Einstein graduated, he was unemployed for two years. Finally, a friend's father got him a job as a Swiss patent clerk. It was there, working in a patent office, where he created his revolutionary scientific theories. Albert Einstein went on to become one of the greatest scientists of the twentieth century. To this day, he is known as the father of modern physics.

Einstein was always looking for new ways to conquer old problems. He knew we can't solve our problems with the same thinking that creates them. "We have to learn to think in a new way," he declared in his 1955 Manifesto.[1] Einstein believed that we must break from old traditions and look outside the conventional box in order to overcome our present difficulties. The best chance we have at solving a problem involves approaching it from a fresh perspective.

The Grand Contradiction is our greatest philosophical problem. It tells us that something is wrong when we start reasoning according to a secular agenda. As long as we follow our most basic and proven rules of reasoning (like the law of noncontradiction and the rule against circular reasoning), the Grand Contradiction is completely unacceptable. It's absurd for us to break our rules in order to establish the very rules we break.

Therefore, in the spirit of Einstein, we must challenge the traditional assumptions of Western philosophy. Reason calls us to do this very thing. And we mustn't settle for the old ways of thinking. This would be nothing more than fallacy (an *argumentum ad antiquitatem*, which is an appeal to tradition). No. We must set aside our biases, open our minds and follow reason wherever it leads.

QUICKSAND

When I was a child my favorite movie was *The Beastmaster*. It was about a barbarian who has psychic powers. He could control the behavior of animals. In one scene, the Beastmaster fell into quicksand. Squirming to get out, he only sank faster. Finally, he called on the help of two nearby ferrets. The ferrets gnawed on a tree limb, which conveniently fell next to the sinkhole. At the end of the scene, the Beastmaster's furry little friends saved the day.

The Grand Contradiction reminds me of this quicksand scene. Once someone decides on secular assumptions, they fall into the Grand Contradiction. They might ignore the problem, but ignoring problems is no way to knowledge. If they try to reason their way out, they only make matters worse, sinking deeper into fallacy. They could try to explain the problem away, but this would just heap circular reasoning and other logical fallacies on top of the situation.

For example, Sigmund Freud assumed our religious feelings are just illusions, wishful thinking based on the natural desire for a better father. Consequently, Freud concluded his personal religious experiences are worthless. Freud's skepticism toward religious experiences is common among atheists, agnostics and other secularists.

How did Freud come to his interpretation of religious experiences? Before Freud decided how religious intuitions fit into his pursuit for knowledge, he first had to make some basic assumptions about what knowledge is and how to go about getting it. Freud also had to assume what a religious experience really is, whether it's a natural human feeling or a genuine brush with the supernatural. Since Freud assumed that knowledge is exclusively about physical things and religious experiences are only natural feelings, his secular conclusions appeared reasonable.

But why should we assume knowledge is only about physical things? Why should we assume religious experiences come from natural causes? Do we have a good reason to make these secular assumptions? Absolutely not. Neither reason nor experience necessarily demand we deny what our religious feelings represent. There isn't a contradiction in the thought that religious experiences are genuine encounters with God. And it's easy enough for people to interpret the human experience religiously.

Nevertheless, Freud still insisted on secular assumptions, which entrapped him in the Grand Contradiction. Did Freud try to resolve this contradiction in his thinking? No. Like most secular scientists, Freud simply ignored the Grand Contradiction to get on with the business of science. On his way to solving some psychological problems, Freud failed to engage the greatest of all our problems, the Grand Contradiction. Cherry picking problems to tackle is a logical fallacy. And since when has ignoring a problem led to knowledge?

Can religious skeptics like Freud justify their secular assumptions? Can they offer a solution for their Grand Contradiction? No. This is impossible. And if they try, they sink deeper into the quicksand of logical fallacies.

Before Freud ever reached his skeptical conclusions, he first assumed a particular concept of knowledge (a definition of knowledge biased toward naturalism). But Freud's definition of "knowledge" discriminating against religion is the precise issue in question. And how could Freud or anyone else ever legitimately argue for an assumption about knowledge when they have already assumed the very thing they intend to prove? A direct argument for Freud's assumptions about what is real and true is nothing more than an exercise in circular reasoning. And we all know that circular reasoning is no help to our search for truth.

If Freud's secular assumptions were not justified by way of reason, where did his skepticism come from? Was it learned at a young age, taught to him by his parents and his teachers? Did he find religious people annoying and blame religion for it? Whatever the cause, it surely wasn't reasonable. Reasoning according to learned prejudices is nothing more than a logical fallacy (an appeal to authority as the philosophers call it). And a decision based on personal feelings is also a fallacy (an appeal to emotion). Bias against religion always emerges from fallacies like these. Obviously, logical fallacies are not the way to knowledge either.

The quicksand Freud found himself in is the same for all who reason according to secular assumptions. The moment they begin reasoning, they create a self-refuting contradiction. They break the very rules of reason they intend to uphold. Now, they might ignore this problem, but ignoring problems does not lead to knowledge. They could try to justify their position, but heaping fallacies on top of circular reasoning is not the way to knowledge either.

What we learn from Freud's example is there's absolutely nothing reasonable about doubting our religious intuitions. On the contrary, doubting our religious experiences leads us straight into the Grand Contradiction. And if people try to reason their way out of this trap, they just make matters worse, sinking deeper into logical fallacies. Secular philosophers and scientists create for themselves a philosophical trap from which there is no escape.

HELP FROM THE OUTSIDE

The Beastmaster needed help from the outside, something on sure footing, to pull him out of the quicksand. Likewise, the only way for us to escape the Grand Contradiction is for someone (or something) greater than ourselves to extend us help. Actively reasoning with a secular agenda only sinks us deeper into the Grand Contradiction. We must be still and passively wait for help. And when it comes, we must receive it.

Saint Augustine wrote about this need for help from the outside. He believed our greatest truths are not the product of human reasoning. Instead, they are revealed to us by God. "We believe in God's Word so that we can understand all else," he said.[2] Augustine's journey toward knowledge began with basic truths revealed by Scripture.

Augustine also taught that faith is a gift from God. It's not a logical conclusion of the human will. Rather, faith is the response to a work of God within our hearts and minds. Faith begins with an unmerited, involuntary feeling, which compels people to believe. Ultimately, God is the direct cause of a person's faith.

Christian faith is based entirely on God's work. God revealed basic truths in the Bible. And God compels us to trust Scripture by producing a personal religious experience within our consciousness. Sure, we can choose whether to heed these feelings or not. But the grounds for religious faith, the ultimate cause, has absolutely nothing to do with human reasoning. And it's a good thing too. For logic tells us this is exactly the sort of outside help we need to overcome the Grand Contradiction.

THE RIGHT TOOL

It's always important to use the right tool for a particular job. One day I discovered my bathroom toilet was leaking. To solve the problem, I had to replace the water line that runs from the floor up to the reservoir. Now, I'm no plumber, but at the time the problem seemed like a quick fix.

However, I didn't have the tool I needed to fix the leak. A small plumber's wrench would have made the job easy. Instead, I used the only tool I had: pliers. About an hour later, after stripping the threads off the fitting, I finally yanked the old tube out of the toilet.

I'm definitely not what you call a handyman. But I know the right tool is necessary for effectively handling any job. Each tool is different, with its own special purpose. And if we use the wrong tool, we usually make our problems worse.

The same is true in our journey for knowledge. Reason is a powerful tool for discovering truth and avoiding falsehood. But it's not for every job. Human reasoning can't justify its own assumptions in a straightforward manner. Nor can reason directly assure us that our search for truth is moving in the right direction. At the beginning of our journey, we need a different tool for the job of starting properly. Otherwise we wind up with the Grand Contradiction.

Why does the Grand Contradiction form? Because people assume that all our beliefs represent human thoughts about the natural world.

People think all our assumptions are based on natural feelings. And the rules of reasoning say, "We must test our human thoughts and scrutinize our natural feelings." We must always check our natural beliefs, supporting them with arguments and evidence. This is what reasoning is all about.

At the same time, we can't directly confirm our most basic assumptions about truth and reality are correct. So, we must give them a free pass. But our rules say we shouldn't do this. Natural human beliefs are fallible, prone to error. They demand supporting arguments and evidence. Yet we have none to offer for an assumption. Thus, we break our proven rules of reason the moment we make an assumption to begin reasoning. This is the root cause of the Grand Contradiction.

But what if naturalists are wrong? What if our mental activity isn't always natural? What if we have another tool in the toolbox? To Augustine's point: What if a dependable God of superior intelligence shared some basic truths with us? And what if, deep within our hearts and minds, God produced the faith that leads us to believe in this revelation? If these things exist, we would have a tool with all the makings to overcome the Grand Contradiction.

Why? Because our Natural Need for Evidence is fitting, so long as we are dealing with "natural" beliefs. Natural human beliefs require a natural human justification. But human thoughts about familiar things are inadequate for justifying a supernaturally-caused belief about unusual things. Natural reasoning simply doesn't apply when understanding something not "natural." Human ideas don't help us make sense of things that aren't "human." Simply put, natural human reasoning is an inappropriate tool for justifying religious faith caused by a supernatural work of God.

These limitations of our human reasoning shouldn't worry us. On the contrary, we should be grateful God assists us in our pursuit for truth the moment we need the most help. If faith in a religious revelation is directly caused by an act of God, then faith has already achieved a higher form of justification. Since supernatural faith isn't based on natural human thoughts, it's no longer appropriate to seek a lesser human justification. Because God is a being of greater power and intelligence, the supernatural justification God provides is far superior to any reason the human mind could ever offer.

And we need to simply receive this kind of faith. If we try to reason about it, we only taint the greater justification with the lesser. To substitute a supernatural justification with a natural one only injects human bias and error into the grounds of our reasoning. And this would invite the Grand Contradiction back into our search for knowledge.

If any belief legitimately deserves a free pass, it's a bona fide supernatural belief. If any belief automatically deserves our trust without question, it's a supernatural faith in a special revelation. Natural human reason has its limitations, which are clearly marked off when facing a genuine supernatural belief.

Therefore, in theory, something like Augustine's account of faith is exactly what we need to overcome the Grand Contradiction. If we base all our reasoning on a supernatural faith in a special revelation, our burden is finally lifted. We no longer need to justify error-prone assumptions with fallible human reasoning. We can finally rest assured that we are beginning our search for knowledge with the correct assumptions. Why? Because truths revealed by a God of superior intelligence are far greater than any knowledge we could ever discover on our own. Logic tells us that a supernaturally-caused faith in a special revelation along the lines of what Augustine described is the tool we need to finally obtain sound knowledge. If this happens to be a real option for us, the Grand Contradiction would suddenly disappear.

THE RIGHT GOD

Helen Keller had an amazing life story. An illness left her deaf and blind when she was nineteen months old. Despite her challenges, Helen Keller discovered how to spell words. She went on to learn Braille and sign language. Eventually, she read lips and even learned how to talk. She was the first blind and deaf person to earn a college degree. She even became a prolific author and lecturer. Helen Keller amazingly overcame her disabilities.

The story of Helen Keller is inspirational on many levels. Most important, it shows that a person must have both the will and the ability to communicate before communication can take place. Helen Keller worked much harder than most, but it's all the same. Communication requires both the desire to connect with others as well as the ability to do so.

The stirring story of Helen Keller is a great example of the special kind of God we need. Logic tells us the only way to overcome the Grand Contradiction is with help from above, a supernatural faith in a special revelation. Of course, this implies the existence of a god. But we don't need just any god. Logic says we need a special God who genuinely loves people enough to ensure we have access to revealed truths. This God must possess both the desire and the ability to communicate truth to us. God must also encourage us to pursue knowledge by way of reason. The existence of this sort of God is our only hope for escaping the Grand Contradiction.

What if a God like this doesn't exist? Or what if the natural world is all there is? If this were the case, our search for truth would be in shambles. In a godless universe, natural human instincts are what ground knowledge. Natural instincts might promote survival, but nothing in nature assures us instincts lead to "truth" (as we commonly think of it). If all our reasoning rests on natural feelings, feelings which don't necessarily yield truth, then we don't even have a good reason to trust our reasoning.

Nor can primal urges help us make good moral decisions, which are essential for "good" reasoning. More often than not, our natural desires conflict with our moral truths. Absolutely nothing in the theory of naturalistic evolution helps us separate good from bad or learn right from wrong. All we have to work with is the principle of "survival of the fittest." And survival has very little to do with searching for truth. It's far too easy to survive without reasoning correctly or knowing truth.

But deep down inside, we all know "truth" involves much more than surviving as a species. For example, we know there is a clear difference between Mother Teresa and Adolf Hitler. But nothing in nature allows for this moral distinction. If survival is our greatest goal in life, Adolf Hitler turns out more righteous than Mother Teresa! It was Hitler who worked hard to put himself and his Aryan race in a better position for survival. Mother Teresa didn't care about her survival. She only wanted to love others. Should we praise Hitler for following his basic survival instincts? Should we fault Mother Teresa for denying those natural urges?

What we call murder, theft and rape happen all the time among animals. These offenses actually help animals survive! But something within our hearts and minds tell us we are different from the animals. Something deep within says to us, "We shouldn't live like animals." Our hearts call us to be heroes, to occasionally put our lives at risk for a greater good, to help others and to live selfless lives. Nothing in nature justifies this life of altruism, the inspirational life we know is best.

Ultimately, there is a moral dimension to our search for truth. Knowledge is all about the "right" way to believe something. Even naturalists think we ought to reason a certain way. They know we should avoid logical fallacies and self-contradictions. "There is a right and wrong way to reason," naturalists say. But good reasoning is not a prerequisite for survival. And naturalism gives us absolutely no reason to reason responsibly.

Even worse, a naturalist cannot offer us a belief that legitimately deserves a free pass. There is no reason for us to think that any natural human belief deserves a free pass. We all know very well that our natural feelings and human thoughts are prone to error. But what we really need to conquer the Grand Contradiction is a special belief that *rightly* deserves a free pass. Only a supernatural faith in a special revelation from God can offer this.

Therefore, naturalism not only creates the Grand Contradiction, it also destroys the very notions of truth and intellectual responsibility, concepts which are essential to any search for knowledge. Obviously, sound knowledge is utterly impossible if naturalism is true.

THE RIGHT REVELATION

The Detroit Pistons were the Bad Boys, a scrappy professional basketball team that won back-to-back NBA championships in 1989 and 1990. The road to this team's first ring was filled with adversity. After a shocking series of events in 1989, all-star Basketball Hall of Famer Adrian Dantley was traded for Mark Aguirre. Although the trade was questionable at the time, the Pistons went on to win two championships in dramatic fashion.

Adrian Dantley didn't get along with his teammates. He constantly argued with his coach. He wouldn't even speak with team owners. Without question, Adrian Dantley was one of the most talented players ever to play the game. But the Pistons had to put their individual egos aside and work as a team to win a championship. And once Dantley was replaced, the Pistons worked together as a cohesive unit.

The Pistons' amazing championship run reminds me of how all our beliefs must work together as we pursue knowledge. If one of our beliefs contradicts another, then our knowledge is flawed. Our beliefs must mesh, functioning as a unified whole, for us to consistently and coherently make sense of the human experience. Our beliefs must be in full agreement with one another if we are to ever reach sound knowledge.

If we are convinced that Western philosophy and science are valuable practices for discovering truth, then our assumptions must reflect that. If we trust modern science as a source for knowledge, then our assumptions must endorse scientific inquiry. We must ground our search for knowledge with special assumptions that encourage us to reason. Otherwise there will be a conflict between our reasoning and the assumptions we reason by. And how can we possibly overcome the Grand Contradiction by creating another contradiction? We can't have a contradiction between our assumptions and our methods. They must work together as a team.

Because we need a unified team of beliefs, we require a special sort of revelation to ground all knowledge. This revelation must first and foremost encourage the use of human logic and critical reasoning. If the basic teachings of any religious revelation are in conflict with the core norms of Western philosophy, then the revelation is incapable of grounding our sciences. If a revelation's clear message clashes with the scientific method, a contradiction would ensue. If a revelation's teachings discourage us from reasoning when we know reason has value, we would only add another contradiction to our list. Therefore, we need a special revelation that consistently endorses reasonable scientific inquiry.

By extension, any religion that encourages people to reject logic and abandon reason just won't do. It is impossible for us to think "Truth is both rational and irrational," without creating a contradiction. And contradictions are precisely what we are trying to avoid.

THE RIGHT FAITH

Living in central Illinois, I experienced many tornadoes. One day I was driving in the pouring rain when the sirens sounded. I couldn't see a foot ahead of me, but I decided to speed home. Once I reached my apartment, I jumped out of the car and darted for the door. Suddenly, the tree next to me split in half and a large limb fell inches in front of me. My roommate opened the front door as I quickly dodged the limb and ran inside.

Experiencing a tornado helps me understand the special kind of faith we must have to resolve the Grand Contradiction. Jesus said, "The wind blows . . . you hear its sound, but you can't tell where it comes from or where it is going. So it is with everyone born of the Spirit" (John 3:7–8). When you're in a tornado, you can't see the funnel. You don't know where the wind comes from or where it's going. All you know is how the wind feels at that moment. And after the tornado passes, you see its effects. Tornadoes leave devastating, life-changing results. It's interesting that Jesus described supernatural faith in a similar way.

Many religious people say they feel God's Spirit from time to time. Christians talk about the Holy Spirit convicting their hearts. I used to think it was weird to hear people talk about some invisible phantom floating around, causing people to believe in odd things. But surprisingly, logic tells us a convicting spiritual force is precisely what we need to avoid the Grand Contradiction and obtain sound knowledge.

The Holy Spirit is able to create a supernatural belief that rightly deserves a free pass. Having an extraordinary assumption that's caused by God avoids the infinite regress and circular reasoning we learned about in chapter three. Our rules of reasoning say we must justify human ideas and natural instincts with arguments and evidence. However, human thoughts can't help us explain something "not human." Natural logic doesn't apply when trying to understand something "not natural." And since an exceptional belief like this comes from a God of superior intelligence who genuinely cares about our pursuit for truth, we can reasonably trust such a special belief without the assistance of our human reasoning. A supernatural belief caused by the Holy Spirit relieves us of the responsibility to directly judge our assumptions before we begin reasoning.

A special revelation is important, but it isn't enough for us to resolve the Grand Contradiction. We also need a supernatural justification as well. If faith is just a decision of the human will, then even Christians are guilty of the Grand Contradiction! If faith is merely a logical conclusion, then it ultimately depends upon a natural human judgment, which is based on natural feelings and human thoughts. But these are the things reason requires us to scrutinize.

You see, religion that depends on the human will leaves us no better off than if we reasoned by secular assumptions. Beginning our journey for knowledge with natural instincts and human principles is what created the Grand Contradiction in the first place. If faith is just another logical conclusion, then we still have no belief rightly deserving a free pass. If faith is merely a decision of the human will, then the Grand Contradiction still exists.

Considering all this, logic tells us the absolute beginning of knowledge must come from something not natural (that is, supernatural). We must start reasoning with a miraculous mental event. Anything less and we are still trapped in the Grand Contradiction. We mustn't begin reasoning with human assumptions, because they require a human justification we just can't give. Only a supernaturally-caused faith is the kind of belief that rightly deserves a free pass. And we must give a worthy belief a free pass in order to avoid the infinite regress of arguments and all the logical fallacies threatening our first step toward knowledge.

But we don't need some vague, mystical conviction. We need a religious experience that comes along with God's clear revelation. We must have an objective message from God to explicitly teach us about this supernatural justification. Why? Because, from our human point of view, there is no reasonable way to distinguish a natural feeling from a supernatural feeling. We have no scientific test, no reasonable rule, for such a task. As Hume said, "The ultimate springs and principles of the things we experience are totally shut up from human curiosity and enquiry."[3] The only way we can really know that a feeling is supernaturally-caused by God is if God clearly tells us. Anything less is human speculation. How could we possibly know anything about a genuine supernatural feeling unless it was clearly revealed to us?

OUR HISTORY

Now, just because we need something doesn't mean we have it. We need a supernatural faith in a special revelation from a God who has both the desire and the ability to communicate truth. These things theoretically avoid the Grand Contradiction and make sound knowledge possible. But do we actually have them? Does a supernaturally-caused faith, a belief that rightly deserves a free pass, exist? Do we have a genuine, objective revelation from God at our fingertips?

Sound knowledge is only possible if we have these things. And if we happen to have sound knowledge, it logically follows that we must also have a supernatural faith in a special revelation grounding this knowledge. So, the next logical question is "Do we have sound knowledge?"

It seems like we have sound knowledge. Our scientific knowledge appears sound. Even the staunchest of atheistic scientists claim their reasoning is sound. And why shouldn't they? Scientific knowledge allows us to accurately predict, even control, nature. The technological advances we receive from science give us many modern conveniences and a substantially higher quality of life. If sound knowledge exists at all, then surely Western science is an instance of it.

Keeping this in mind, it's fascinating to see that the history of Western science confirms everything our logic tells us. Since the beginning of time, people from all cultures have studied nature. However, Western science (as a formal discipline) began with the ancient Greeks. Early Greek philosophers encouraged the use of reason in their search for truth. Plato focused on satisfying our Natural Need for Evidence. He assumed that all our beliefs must be backed by good arguments in order to count as knowledge. This assumption left old superstitions behind and ushered in a new scientific method for pursuing truth.

However, most Greek philosophers also imposed a secular agenda on their pursuit for knowledge. Protagoras assumed "Man is the measure of all things" as the guiding principle for Western philosophy. Ancient Greeks began with secular assumptions about truth and reality. And once the Skeptics questioned these assumptions, the Grand Contradiction became apparent. So long as our Natural Need for Evidence was paired with Protagoras's principle, sound knowledge became impossible.

In this environment, science stagnated. Ancient Greeks spent centuries arguing over whether earth, wind or fire was the most important element. Skeptics wondered if we should even seek knowledge in the first place. Early philosophers had the intellect and the will for scientific inquiry, but they lacked the necessary guidance from outside themselves. They didn't have a special revelation to point their search in the right direction. What resulted was a chaotic hodgepodge of traditions, all groping for a way to understand a world without a clear revelation from God.

It wasn't until AD fourth century when things started to change. Emperor Constantine converted to Christianity and citizens of the Roman Empire began mixing Greek philosophy with Christian thought. Later, Augustine rejected Protagoras's principle and merged Plato's thought with the teachings of the Bible. At this point, Western science had all the elements necessary to finally obtain sound knowledge.

But something went wrong. As the Christian church grew in power, its leaders became corrupt. For personal gain and other unreasonable motives, various members of the clergy placed restrictions on humanity's pursuit for knowledge. They eventually condemned the theories of free-thinking scientists like Galileo. Some scientific progress was made within the halls of medieval universities. But by and large the Dark Ages are called "dark" for good reason. Sadly, the Catholic Church had the right foundation for knowledge, but some powerful members of the clergy ultimately sabotaged humanity's fast track toward sound knowledge.

It wasn't until the Renaissance that Western science suddenly advanced by leaps and bounds. Renaissance scientists based their methods on biblical truths. Scientists such as Copernicus, Kepler and Galileo believed in the God of the Bible, a God who created a universe governed by natural laws. They understood that religion opens the door to consistent, comprehensive knowledge. Francis Bacon, the founder of the scientific method, summed up modern science's need for a religious foundation when he wrote, "A little philosophy inclines our minds to atheism; but depth in philosophy brings our minds to religion."[4]

These scientists set aside their biases and personal desires, following reason wherever it led. The combination of biblical truths with objective reasoning freed them to pursue sound knowledge with astonishing success. If there's one thing we learn from the Scientific Revolution it's this: Western science did not rapidly progress until free human reasoning combined with supernatural faith in a special revelation.

You see, ancient Greek philosophers were so busy thinking about what direction their journey should take, they could never get down to the business of science. Egyptians, Indians, Persians and Chinese all made various contributions, but their assumptions weren't able to launch their science into the modern era. The Roman Catholic clergy had the right assumptions for the job, but some of them stifled reason in favor of misguided religious traditions. It wasn't until truths from a special revelation were combined with impartial reasoning that science magnificently flourished.

But this great achievement didn't last long. Soon after, proponents of the secular agenda hijacked Western science. In 1859 Charles Darwin published *On the Origin of Species*, and the supernatural basis for science was quickly forgotten. Make no mistake, all scientists (even atheists) retained distinctly Christian assumptions. Biblical beliefs like "The natural world exists independent of the senses," "Our senses reliably represent reality," "The natural world is intelligible," "Reasoning is worthwhile," "Knowledge is useful," etc. still ground Western science. But many scientists ultimately forgot these foundational principles came from a religious source (see Gen. 1:1-2:3; 1 Kings 4:29-34; Ps. 8; Prov. 3:13-20, 4:7; Jer. 33:25-26).

In the modern era, secular scientists ignore the indisputable fact it was God's Word that revealed basic scientific truths to us, thereby making our sciences possible. What the ancient Greeks could not establish on their own, modern scientists have taken for granted.

Nonreligious scientists reject the reality of miracles. Some think religion is a useless illusion. What they have done is replaced God's Word with man-made assumptions. They have exchanged the greater for the lesser. Thus, the Grand Contradiction made its way back into our search for knowledge. Nonreligious scientists and philosophers thought they were liberating themselves by promoting a secular agenda for knowledge. But in reality, they just trapped themselves with self-refuting contradictions, destroying all hope for sound knowledge.

To this day, secular philosophers and scientists still try to deny these historical facts. They argue that successes of modern science prove religion's uselessness and irrelevance. But nothing could be further from the truth. You see, Western science didn't make substantial progress until it received Christian assumptions and paired biblical truths with reasonable thinking. Even now, secular scientists depend upon the very principles of reasoning that God first revealed to humanity thousands of years ago. Therefore, the successes of modern science don't show us that religion is unnecessary. On the contrary, scientific progress in the modern era proves we must begin our pursuit of knowledge with a special revelation. To think otherwise is to ignore the historical roots of Western science.

History proves that we need a special revelation to put our search for truth on the right course. God, through the Bible, revealed the most basic assumptions of science: Nature exists independent of our senses, nature is orderly and intelligible, our senses are reliable, people have dominion over nature, scientific study is beneficial, the pursuit of knowledge is good, etc. Ironically, if Western philosophers and scientists reject God's Word, they deny the very assumptions of their reasoning. In this way, history confirms what our logic tells us: We must begin our journey for truth with a supernatural faith in a special revelation; otherwise, sound knowledge is impossible.

FOLLOWING REASON

When I was eighteen, I owned an old car. One day it wouldn't start. I had no idea what the problem was. Before long, my dad came along, opened the hood and looked over the engine. "It might be the alternator, or the battery," he mumbled as he walked over to his toolbox. Next thing I knew, my dad was under the hood, explaining to me the inner workings of my car's engine.

Back then I didn't know much about cars. When my car broke down, I didn't have the faintest idea where to begin. It would have taken me hours just to find the right tools for the job. What I desperately needed was someone with more knowledge than I had to give me some guidance. I needed an experienced mechanic to point me in the right direction. Only when I had the proper instruction could I solve my car problems.

This is the situation we are all in. We all need a bit of guidance to set our pursuit for knowledge on the right track. Without the proper instruction from someone more knowledgeable than ourselves, we flounder. We can design our schemes and form our theories, but we aren't sure our reasoning is headed in the right direction.

Sound logic (that is, logic based on fair, open-minded assumptions that allow for a solution to the Grand Contradiction) says we need a supernatural faith in a special revelation to ensure we are on the right path. Anything else and we get trapped inside the Grand Contradiction. And the history of Western science confirms this truth of reason. Because modern science is based on the revealed truths of Scripture. Paradoxically, our natural sciences necessarily require supernatural assumptions. To deny this fact not only denies history, it also rejects sound logic.

The philosopher W.V.O. Quine once said, "Science is not committed to the physical, whatever that means."[5] His point was clear. We should be open-minded, following reason wherever it leads. This is always true, even if reason leads us where we don't want to go. And when it comes to solving our biggest problem, the Grand Contradiction, both reason and experience point us to one conclusion: Sound knowledge begins with a supernatural faith in a special revelation. Since we know we have sound knowledge, it follows that we must also have a genuine revelation from God grounding this knowledge.

5

The Search

God's Word Is The Best And Only Basis For Our Sound Knowledge

STARTING A SEARCH WELL

The Goonies is a classic movie about a group of kids in search of pirate's treasure. The kids stumble upon a map filled with riddles. But early in their journey the children weren't sure where to begin. Without knowing the location of their map's starting point, it was impossible to follow the clues to One-Eyed Willie's treasure.

Luckily, the Goonies also found a gold doubloon with three small holes in it. Once Mikey peered through the doubloon and matched its holes with surrounding landmarks, the Goonies discovered the location where they could finally begin their journey.

The greatest of all Goonies adventures teaches us a valuable lesson about pursuing knowledge. Finding the right place to start is essential for any successful search. Presently, we are searching for a solution to our greatest philosophical problem, the Grand Contradiction. Logic shows us only supernatural faith in a special revelation gives a path to sound knowledge. And the history of Western science confirms this truth, because, as we learned in the previous chapter, modern science is based on truths revealed by God's Word, the Bible.

But one question still remains. Are the Judeo-Christian Scriptures the best and only starting point for knowledge? We know that Western science is founded on God's Word. But this historical fact doesn't automatically guarantee that Christianity is the only religion leading to sound knowledge. Nor does it necessarily imply that Christian beliefs are any truer than other religions.

Which sacred text is best suited to ground all our knowledge without creating contradictions in our thinking? To answer this question, we must review all the world religions. Once we narrow down the possibilities and discern the best revelation for our task at hand, we will reasonably determine the optimal revelation to ground all knowledge. In this way, we can prove the truthfulness of one religion above all others, and finally discover the best place to begin our search for sound knowledge.

PROCESS OF ELIMINATION

My wife watches a reality TV show called *The Bachelor*. It's about one man who simultaneously dates twenty-five different women. Each week the Bachelor hands out roses to the women he wants to keep around. If a girl doesn't receive a rose, she packs her bags and goes home. Through this process of elimination, the Bachelor narrows down his choices in order to find that one woman best suited for him.

Our search for knowledge calls for a similar process of elimination. We need to find the best revelation for the job of grounding all knowledge contradiction-free. And for all intents and purposes, the religion that best explains our sound knowledge is the superior religion of truth.

But remember, we need three things to avoid the Grand Contradiction. First, we need a special revelation. Second, our revelation must teach us about a supernaturally-caused faith. Third, all this logically implies the existence of a higher intelligence (call it God), who possesses both the power and desire to reveal truth and communicate with us. Only these three things together can give us an extraordinary belief that rightly deserves a free pass. Only this situation can save us from the Grand Contradiction.

Considering this logic, the aim of comparing our world's religions is not to pit one faith against another. Nor is it to make ancient teachings more palatable and relevant. And we surely aren't out to change a religion's teachings to our liking. We are simply looking for that special revelation best suited to avoid the Grand Contradiction and coherently ground all knowledge. For us to determine this, we must ask four simple questions:

1. Do we have available to us a real, supernatural revelation?
2. Do a religion's prophets give us miraculous evidence?
3. Does the revelation encourage us to use logic and reason consistently?
4. Does the revelation teach us about supernaturally-caused faith?

If we answer "No" to any of these, the religion in question does not offer us what we need. As we discovered in the last chapter, we need a genuine revelation from God, because a book penned by mere men can't offer help from the outside. We also need a prophet who performed miracles, because only supernatural evidence can reasonably confirm a revelation is supernatural. We need a religious text that encourages us to reason consistently, because reason must always guide our pursuit for knowledge. And we need teachings about a supernatural faith, because we have no other way to reasonably distinguish natural beliefs from supernatural beliefs. If a religion doesn't offer us all these things, the Grand Contradiction will persist.

A REAL REVELATION

A boy named Siddhartha Gautama was born into a royal family around 500 BC. Legend has it his mother dreamed about a white elephant entering inside her the night the boy was conceived. The boy grew up in Nepal and lived in a palace as a prince. There he was sheltered from all of life's troubles.

But when Gautama turned twenty-nine years old, he ventured outside the palace walls and discovered a world filled with suffering people. From that moment on, Siddhartha Gautama rejected his wealth. One evening, he sat down under a tree, vowing not to stand until he discovered life's greatest truths. About seven weeks later, the young man rose to accept his new name, Buddha (which means the Enlightened One). Buddha became the founder of Buddhism.

Buddhism is a good example of a world religion that offers people insightful teachings. Its sacred texts are filled with practical wisdom. However, our ultimate task is to overcome the Grand Contradiction and find the *best* explanation for our sound knowledge. Therefore, we are most concerned with a real, supernatural revelation. So, our question is this: Are we dealing with a real revelation from God here?

Buddhism and other Eastern religions only offer us philosophies that originated from the minds of other men and women. Most Buddhists think either God doesn't exist or God isn't important to our search for knowledge. For example, Tenzin Gyatso, the 14th Dalai Lama of Tibetan Buddhism, openly denies the existence of a loving, powerful Creator who reveals truth to us.[1] Consequently, Buddhism cannot offer us what we are looking for.

Religions based on human thoughts and natural feelings don't just come from the East. Liberal religions in the West offer the same sort of humanistic beginnings. Liberal scholars deny the reality of miracles. They reject the Bible's inspiration. But without miracles and inspired prophets, we no longer have a clear, objective revelation on our hands. A book written by mere men just won't do. And any revelation that is stripped of the supernatural can't help us overcome the Grand Contradiction. Why? Because humanistic religions can't give us a supernatural belief that rightly deserves a free pass.

Eastern religions and liberal denominations fail to offer us a real revelation. Their teachings are based on human thoughts and natural feelings. And if they claim to offer some vague, supernatural experience, we have no reasonable way to confirm that God is behind it. Humanistic religions just won't do. They begin with natural human reasoning, which is precisely what got us into the Grand Contradiction in the first place.

MIRACULOUS EVIDENCE

The Isabella Stewart Gardner Museum in Boston, Massachusetts is the location of one of the greatest heists in history. On March 18, 1990, two men disguised as police officers coaxed security guards to let them enter the building. The thieves tied up the guards and stole thirteen pieces of rare artwork. With stolen treasures valued at five hundred million dollars, the Gardner Heist is the largest private property theft in history. To this day, the case remains unsolved.

These two thieves were successful because they didn't leave a shred of evidence behind. Detectives scoured the museum but couldn't find any evidence to help their investigation. These detectives might have been brilliant sleuths. But they weren't given enough evidence to make an informed decision. And when evidence is lacking, human reason can no longer assist us in our search for truth.

The Gardner Heist a good example of how important evidence is for our journey. We must have a sufficient amount of tangible evidence to draw a reasonable conclusion. Otherwise, we have nothing to seriously reason about.

And regarding our search for a solution to the Grand Contradiction, we need evidence indicating that something supernatural is at work. We need to see supernatural characteristics when reading a revelation. We need a prophet to perform amazing miracles. Why? Because supernatural evidence demonstrates a revelation's supernatural origin.

Both the style and the substance of a prophet's message are telling pieces of evidence. Unusual topics, puzzling teachings and claims of divine inspiration all go a long way to show a prophet's message is truly from God. Amazingly consistent themes and reconcilable inconsistencies might also indicate that something both reasonable and supernatural is at work. It's reasonable to expect a revelation from extraordinary origins to offer us an extraordinary message.

On the other hand, a simple writing containing obvious errors and familiar themes is what we'd expect from a human author. A book that appears humanly likely comes from the minds of mere men and women. Without extraordinary characteristics, we have no reason to think a religious writing is truly from God.

Miracles also serve as clear evidence demonstrating a prophet's divine authority. Unmistakable miracle working grabs our attention and proves that something supernatural is really at work. Without miracles, we have no tangible evidence supporting a prophet's claims.

An unusual message along with amazing miracles are the sort of evidence we need to see that a religious revelation is really a supernatural message from God. Without such evidence, we have no reason to think a sacred text is a genuine revelation.

Whether or not someone assumes miracles are possible (or even reasonable to believe in) is neither here nor there. The point is this: A truly supernatural revelation must exhibit supernatural characteristics, and its authors must perform miracles. Otherwise, we have no evidence to reason about. And we can't reasonably believe something without the proper evidence to do so. As a general rule, the natural will always appear natural. And the supernatural must appear supernatural for us to logically discern God is at work.

David Hume famously assumed, "It's more reasonable to doubt a miracle occurred than trust a person's testimony of the marvelous."[2] Based on our experiences from daily living, Hume had a point here. Most people don't see miracles happen every day. And by definition, a miracle is an unusual, highly improbable event that breaks the regular laws of nature.

However, the problem with Hume's assumptions about knowledge is that he failed to understand one thing. Miracles are the clear evidence we need to reasonably infer that a religious text is, in fact, supernatural. And the greater the miracle, the more obvious a supernatural force is at work. Paradoxically, the more marvelous the miracle, the more reasonable religious faith becomes. This is true because clear violations of our natural laws are precisely what show us that something beyond nature is at work. And without an unmistakable miracle, we have no good reason to think a prophet offers us a message from God.

Hume made a good point about testing a prophet's message. But he failed on one count. He offered us no solution to our greatest problem, the Grand Contradiction. After struggling with the inconsistencies of his reasoning, Hume eventually gave up, deciding to just ignore all his logical fallacies. He overlooked the problem and chose to distract himself with food, friends and backgammon games.[3] But since when has ignoring our problems and distracting ourselves with games led to knowledge?

If we are going to discover a solution to the Grand Contradiction, we must allow ourselves to look for miracles among the prophets of our world's religions. If we don't have miracles, then we don't have evidence to reason about. Therefore, by assuming (like Hume did) that miracles are either impossible or unreasonable, skeptics destroy all hope for a supernatural faith in a special revelation. This ultimately makes sound knowledge impossible, thereby denying the sound knowledge we know we have.

Concerning our search at hand, when we look for miracles among the founders of our world's religions, we are, by and large, disappointed. Many religions originated from self-proclaimed prophets who failed to offer us miraculous evidence backing their claims.

The Unification Church is a good example of an Eastern religion offering us no evidence whatsoever. Reverend Sun Myung Moon wrote a book called *Divine Principle*. In this sacred text, Moon claims the Christ will return to earth in the twentieth century. In 1992, Reverend Moon publicly declared that he and his wife were "the Messiah," the True Parents of all humanity.[4] Now, Reverend Moon gave us some fantastic claims, but they are without a fantastic reason to trust him. Moon offered not one miracle to support his claim that he was a prophet with a supernatural message.

There are plenty of other examples of miraculous talk without the miraculous evidence. L. Ron Hubbard, the founder of Scientology, taught that we all came from a race of gods called Thetans. Mary Baker Eddy, the mother of Christian Science, claimed she was divinely inspired by God. But did either of these founders give us a miraculous reason to believe? No.

Most religions make fantastic claims about reality but don't give us good reasons to think they are actually true. If a prophet doesn't work miracles, we can't very well reason about his or her message. If prophets demand we trust them blindly, then we could be duped into believing anything. A religion without miracles gives no reasonable assurance that its teachings are from God. And we can't just abandon our Natural Need for Evidence when it matters most. Miraculous evidence displaying the supernatural nature of a religious revelation is necessary for our escape from the Grand Contradiction.

CONSISTENT TEACHINGS

A boy named Muhammad was born in present-day Saudi Arabia around AD 570. At the age of forty, Muhammad was praying in a cave when an angel appeared to him. During this encounter, the angel revealed to Muhammad what is now known as the Quran. In this way, Muslims believe the religion of Islam was born.

Initially, the Quran seems to have all the makings of that special revelation we need. The prophet Muhammad claimed he received a genuine revelation from a god (Allah). But does the Quran encourage us to reason consistently about all things, even our religious beliefs?

Sadly, Islam's teachings on our pursuit for knowledge contradict our proven scientific method. When it comes to the most important of all beliefs, religious faith, the Quran calls people to abandon all reasoning. Islam teaches that we must betray our Natural Need for Evidence and irrationally trust Muhammad. The Quran puts it this way:

> Even if Allah sent down angels or if dead people spoke, people still wouldn't believe unless Allah pleases. Therefore, whomever Allah intends that He would guide him aright, He expands his breast for Islam, and whomsoever He intends that He should cause him to err, He makes his breast straight and narrow.[5]

According to Muhammad, Allah directly causes people to believe religiously. Consequently, the Quran teaches Muslims to blindly trust Muhammad. "Signs and wonders are of no use," the Quran says.[6] Islam is telling us we shouldn't look for evidence to support a prophet's testimony. The Quran claims it's a supernatural revelation from Allah, but

Muhammad offered not one shred of supernatural evidence to support this claim.

This teaching is not only suspect. It creates a serious logical problem. On one hand, Islam encourages our Natural Need for Evidence, promoting reason and science as the proven way to truth. On the other hand, Islam says we must forgo reasoning, denying our Natural Need for Evidence when it matters most (when it comes to our religious beliefs). To say "we must reason" and "we mustn't reason" at the same time is a clear contradiction. Simply put, Islam encourages inconsistent reasoning (if any reasoning at all). And since when have contradictions and inconsistent reasoning led to knowledge?

Remember, miracles are the evidence we need to reasonably gauge the truthfulness of a prophet's message. The fact that a prophet doesn't offer us miracles and discourages us to seek miracles proves that he or she isn't concerned about reasoning consistently according to evidence. Prophets who don't offer miracles would rather us abandon all logic and naively embrace their message than uphold our proven rules of reasoning. It's clear that such illogical demands are not only unreasonable, they are intellectually irresponsible.

Similarly, cults that claim to be Christian promote the same sort of inconsistent reasoning. Mormonism offers us a prophet named Joseph Smith. Smith even performed a few miracles here and there. But his teachings fail to encourage consistent reasoning. In *Doctrine and Covenants*, Smith tells us that our feelings are the ultimate judge of truth:

> Behold, you have not understood. I say to you, that you must study . . . then you must ask me [God] if it's right. And if it's right I will cause your bosom to burn within you. Therefore, you shall feel that it is right. But if it isn't right, you shall have no such feelings.[7]

As we read the books of different religions, how do we know they are true? Smith taught that our "bosom will burn" when we read truth. Clearly, this method for discerning truth and avoiding falsehood contradicts the proven practices of Western philosophy and science. Symptoms of heartburn are not a truth test endorsed by modern science.

Even some mainstream Christian denominations compromise our pursuit of knowledge by defining faith in irrational terms. Soren Kierkegaard introduced the idea of a "leap of faith" to the Christian church. Since then, many Christians have separated "head" knowledge from feelings of the "heart." "Faith is a matter of the heart," they say. This sort of irrational faith only adds fuel to the Grand Contradiction. Just like other religions and cults, irrational brands of Christianity abandon reason when we need it most, thereby creating a contradiction between our proven tests of reason and the inconsistent way they approach religious faith. And the whole point of our search for a revelation is to avoid contradictions, not create more.

THE LAST RELIGION STANDING

When I was growing up, I loved watching action movies. Characters like *Die Hard*'s John McClane, *Lethal Weapon*'s Martin Riggs and John Rambo always defeated the bad guys and saved the day. They single-handedly took on armies, leaving piles of bodies in their wake. And at the end of the movies, these heroes were always the last men standing.

These action heroes remind me of our search for the best religious revelation to ground all our knowledge and finally defeat the Grand Contradiction. By process of elimination, one religious tradition meets all our requirements. We need a real revelation, one that appears supernatural and comes with miraculous evidence. We also require a revelation that consistently encourages us to reason about all things, even itself. A special revelation like this is what we need to overcome our contradictions and explain the sound knowledge we know we have.

After a thorough search, only one religion offers us everything we need to begin our journey toward sound knowledge. Orthodox Christianity is the last religion standing.

Every other religion inconsistently applies our proven rules of reasoning, thereby creating self-refuting contradictions. Eastern religions like Taoism tell us to "give up learning."[8] Even some Christians say we should shut off our brains in order to trust God. To say that we must reason and give evidence for our beliefs but fail to reason and give evidence for our religious beliefs is a double standard, a contradiction that is the height of intellectual hypocrisy. And this is precisely what we are trying to avoid: contradictions in our thinking.

The message of Jesus Christ as taught by the early Christian church is the only revelation able to give us everything we need to overcome the Grand Contradiction. It passes all our logical tests with flying colors. Let's review them:

1. Do we have available to us a real, supernatural revelation?
2. Do a religion's prophets give us miraculous evidence?
3. Does the revelation encourage us to use logic and reason consistently?
4. Does the revelation teach us about supernaturally-caused faith?

1. Do we have available to us a real, supernatural revelation? God's Word, the Bible, claims it is a real revelation. The apostle Peter wrote, "No prophecy of Scripture came about by a man's own thinking. Prophecy never had its origin in the human will. Men spoke from God as they were carried along by the Holy Spirit" (2 Peter 1:20–21). Paul put it this way, "The gospel I preached is not something that man made up. I did not receive it from any man, nor was I taught it; rather, I received it by revelation from Jesus Christ" (Gal. 1:11–12). And Jesus Christ proclaimed, "My teaching is not my own. It comes from Him who sent me" (John 7:16).

God's Word is also filled with peculiar teachings beyond human understanding. Doctrines like the Trinity, Christ's incarnation, our election to salvation and biblical inspiration are paradoxical revelations that challenge our notion of common sense. But the oddness of such foreign teachings doesn't necessarily count against their truthfulness. On the contrary, these teachings are clear marks of transcendence, confirming that Scripture is a revelation truly from a supernatural source.

2. Do a religion's prophets give us miraculous evidence? The Bible is supported by miraculous historical evidence. Jesus Christ fulfilled all the old prophecies about the Messiah (see Gen. 3:15; 2 Sam. 7; Ps. 118:22–23). He raised the dead and healed hundreds of people.

And who could forget the greatest miracle of all? Jesus Christ came back to life from the dead (the resurrection)! The most spectacular and inexplicable miracle of all time was performed in the crowded capital of Jerusalem during the Jewish Passover festival. This location and timing ensured that a maximum number of impartial witnesses were in attendance for the death and resurrection of Jesus Christ. In both quality and quantity, the historical evidence for Christ's resurrection far surpasses that of any other religion's purported miracles. And no other religion can claim its founding prophet rose from the dead.

3. Does the revelation encourage us to use logic and reason consistently? The Bible encourages us to consistently reason about all things, even itself. Scripture clearly endorses the scientific study of our natural world. King Solomon applied the scientific method toward understanding nature (1 Kings 4:32–34). And Jesus Christ honored Solomon's scientific achievements (Matt. 12:42). Reason and revelation are in complete agreement concerning the value of the scientific method in our journey toward sound knowledge.

God's Word also teaches us to think critically about our religious beliefs. God told Moses to test the prophets. "How can we know when a message has not been spoken by the LORD?" Moses asked. "If anything a prophet claims does not take place or come true, then it is a message the LORD has not spoken" (Deut. 18:21–22). God also challenges us to test His goodness with our giving. "Test me and see if I will not throw open the floodgates of heaven," God dared Malachi (3:10). Jesus Christ gave an entire sermon on reasons to believe His testimony (John 5:31-47). And Jesus continually invited skeptics to consider His miracles as evidence proving His supernatural origin (Matt. 9:6).

The overall message of Scripture is clear. God calls us to consistently reason about all things, even our religious beliefs. God's Word teaches us to demand miraculous evidence from any self-professing prophet. We must subject all religious claims to our proven tests of reason. And only the Bible meets all our logical requirements for that special revelation we need to overcome the Grand Contradiction. In this way, we can reasonably prove that God's Word is the best explanation for the knowledge we know we have, thereby demonstrating with sound logic that Christianity is the one true religion.

4. Does the revelation teach us about supernaturally-caused faith? One day my wife went on a business trip. When she returned home, she discovered the diamond in her wedding ring was missing. Frantically, she recalled all of the places she visited. She phoned hotels, restaurants and gas stations, asking if anyone found her diamond. Amazingly, a restaurant owner called my wife to tell her it was found! An employee just happened to look down and notice the diamond in a parking lot.

When my wife realized her diamond was missing, she reasoned about all the places it might be. She looked up phone numbers. She made calls. She did everything within her power to find that diamond. But part of her search was entirely out of her control. She put herself in the best situation to find the lost gem, but she still needed help from someone other than herself to track it down.

Our search for a special revelation is no different. Although the Bible passes all our tests of reason with flying colors, we still need God to convict our hearts and make us believe in a supernatural way. This is what supernatural faith is all about. And this is exactly what we need to overcome the Grand Contradiction.

God's Word teaches us about a Holy Spirit who miraculously works within our minds, convicting us and making the truth known (John 16:7–15; 1 Cor. 2:7–16; 1 John 2:26–27). In fact, Scripture teaches that no one can understand God's Word unless the Holy Spirit first does a supernatural work within his or her heart. Paul wrote, "The person without the Spirit does not accept the things that come from the Spirit of God" (1 Cor. 2:14).

Given the Bible's clear teachings on a supernaturally-caused faith, our search is now over. By process of elimination, our comparison of the world's religions confirms what history and logic have demonstrated all along. Sound knowledge begins with God's Word. By all rational accounts, the Bible is the best and only explanation for all the knowledge we know we have.

All we have to do now is merely listen to God's call, heed those mysterious feelings deep within our hearts and accept God's Word as true. And when we respond most reasonably to these religious intuitions, the Grand Contradiction suddenly disappears.

IRRATIONAL REJECTION

At this point we should ask ourselves, "Why do people still reject God's Word?" Sound reasoning leads us to the foot of the cross. And our personal religious experiences compel us to accept the reality of Christ's teachings. By all rational accounts, we should trust our intuitions (especially the religious ones) and take God's Word at face value. We have no good, noncircular reason not to.

But something other than reason (something irrational) nudges people to resist the Holy Spirit's call. Through misguided assumptions and logical fallacies, people trade in the possibility of sound knowledge for the Grand Contradiction. Even though people committed to the secular agenda might feel liberated from things they dislike about organized religion, they have done nothing more than trap themselves in a web of self-contradictions the moment they refuse to believe in the one thing necessary for overcoming the Grand Contradiction—the message of Jesus Christ and his Apostles. And we must admit that settling for the self-refuting Grand Contradiction instead of a coherent explanation for our sound knowledge is the most unreasonable of all decisions.

ARE WE TRAPPED?

As we conclude our search, a philosopher might ask, "Aren't you searching for a solution to the Grand Contradiction with reasoning still based on contradictions?" In any search, we don't yet have what we are looking for. This is also true regarding our search for a solution to the Grand Contradiction.

As we seek a way to escape our contradictions, we are unavoidably depending on reasoning still plagued by the Grand Contradiction.

But we have to start our journey toward sound knowledge somewhere. And we must try to find some way to escape all the self-refuting contradictions that come along with the sort of reasoning we learned as children. Therefore, we must begin where we're at and work toward a better situation. This is the way life works. This is how we grow and better ourselves as people. Our search for knowledge is no different.

So, by trial and error, we must piece together different combinations of assumptions, hoping we might soon stumble across a coherent worldview that best explains all the knowledge we know we have. Admittedly, our search doesn't begin perfectly. But it's still the best shot we have at freedom from all contradictions.

The good news is this: Once we discover the right mix of assumptions along with the best religious revelation for the job, the Grand Contradiction suddenly disappears. And when we finally recognize that God's Word grounds all knowledge as our ultimate authority on truth, sound knowledge (knowledge free from all contradictions) is instantly within our grasp.

6

The Case

Given The Right Assumptions, Christian Faith Is Reasonable

THE RECIPE

When I was growing up, my grandma always came over for Thanksgiving dinner. She brought a variety of baked goodies, including her tasty pumpkin roll. One year the pumpkin roll didn't turn out right. It was dry and hard. Grandma swore she used the same recipe as always, but something was off this time. By the end of our meal, my grandma was so frustrated with her dessert that she vowed never to make her famous pumpkin roll again.

The funny thing about baking with recipes is dishes don't always turn out as advertised. You can have a perfect recipe for the best cake. But when you're done, the cake doesn't always turn out right. If you add too much of one ingredient or not enough of another, suddenly the perfect recipe doesn't offer what was promised. A great recipe doesn't guarantee great results.

Building a reasonable case for Christianity is like baking with a recipe. On paper is a large pool of evidence supporting Christian truths. Christ's documented miracles, hundreds of fulfilled prophecies, thousands of biblical manuscripts and compelling logical arguments all come together as the perfect recipe for reasonable faith. In both quality and quantity, the historical evidence for Christ's resurrection is superior to the evidence favoring any other world religion.

But when Christians share the evidence, not everyone is convinced. The case isn't always persuasive for skeptics. Christians who expect people to hear their arguments and suddenly convert are often disappointed.

If the case for Christianity is so strong, why do some people still doubt? Doubts could be due to bad reasoning. But most of the time doubt is the conclusion of good reasoning based on bad assumptions. If a skeptic assumes "God doesn't exist" or "Miracles never happen" before he or she reviews the evidence, a Christian's case will always be unconvincing. Things like the incarnation (a person who is both God and man) and Christ's resurrection (Jesus coming back to life from the dead) appear as nonsense so long as someone interprets the evidence through the prism of secular assumptions.

The fact that people aren't always persuaded by the evidence shouldn't discourage Christians. Because the goal of any case for Christianity is not to convert skeptics. The role of arguments and evidence is merely to show that faith is entirely reasonable under the right circumstances. As long as people begin reasoning with fair, open-minded assumptions, history and logic always offer us the sufficient evidence we need to reasonably conclude Jesus Christ is the Son of God. Therefore, given the best assumptions (which are assumptions that allow for a solution to the Grand Contradiction), faith is clearly more reasonable than doubt. The goal of any apology, any case for Christianity, is to prove nothing more, nothing less.

It's strange that people put higher stakes on debate. Some Christians want to "prove" God exists, regardless of what assumptions people bring to the conversation. And many atheists naively insist "There is no evidence for God," without engaging how assumptions control interpretations of the evidence. But in the end, arguments never cause people to believe. Evidence doesn't force skeptics into assent.

If arguments and evidence were all that's needed to coerce people into religion, then faith would ultimately rest on human reasoning. If Christian faith was merely a logical assent to the propositions of Scripture, then faith would amount to an act of the human will. But this is not the essence of true faith. Christian faith is not a logical conclusion of human reasoning!

And it's a good thing too. Because a supernatural faith in a special revelation is precisely what we need to escape the Grand Contradiction.

Christian faith is simply a reasonable response to a supernatural work. Real faith begins with a personal religious experience, a mysterious intuition compelling us to believe the testimony of Scripture is true. And when we heed this call deep within our hearts, sound knowledge suddenly becomes possible.

Therefore, the case for Christianity is out to prove one thing: Given the best assumptions, trusting God's Word is more reasonable than doubt. On the right assumptions, faith in Jesus Christ is entirely reasonable. Reason and revelation are in complete agreement on this matter.

QUALITY EVIDENCE

Mormons claim that an angel appeared to Joseph Smith and disclosed the location of some buried golden plates. As the story goes, Smith retrieved these plates and translated their writings with a magical seer stone. The result was the Book of Mormon, the sacred text for Latter-day Saints.

Do we have a good reason to trust Joseph Smith's claims? Presently, these golden plates are nowhere to be found. And Mormon tradition says only eleven people ever witnessed them. Three cofounders of the religion saw a "vision" of the plates. And the other eight witnesses were family members of both Joseph Smith and cofounder David Whitmer.

If these golden plates were on display in a museum for the world to see, we would have a relic to study. If hundreds of impartial eyewitnesses had seen the plates with their own eyes, we might have a reason to trust Smith's testimony. But without the actual plates or objective testimonies, the case for Mormonism is suspect. This lack of good evidence was the basis for Mark Twain's sarcastic comment, "I could not feel more satisfied if the entire Whitmer family had testified [about the plates]."[1]

Obviously, some types of evidence are better than others. This was David Hume's point when he famously argued against miracles. "No testimony is sufficient to establish a miracle, unless the testimony be of such a kind, that its falsehood would be more miraculous than the miracle which it endeavors to establish."[2] Ironically, Hume echoed the teachings of Scripture here. God told Moses that Israel must test the prophets to ensure that a prophecy is genuine (Deut. 18:21–22). The point is this: We must have a healthy dose of scrutiny when we hear from any self-proclaimed prophet. We need more evidence than a prophet's own testimony or the testimony of his family members.

What we need is tangible, objective evidence. Reason demands that we study evidence like original texts, unearthed artifacts and other relics. At the very least, we need the recorded testimonies of impartial witnesses who clearly don't have ulterior motives.

Regarding a recipe for building a case, there are different ways to present the evidence for Christian faith. Some begin with classical arguments about a First Cause and a Designer. Others reference the Bible as a dependable historical source. In my opinion, a case based on the best evidence will focus on the testimonies of secular historians.

Secular authors from the first and second centuries are as impartial as a witness can get. They were well aware of historical events from the first century. Yet they had no motive for promoting Christianity. In fact, they preferred insulting the religion.

Furthermore, their written testimonies still exist to this day. These manuscripts are on display in some of the world's greatest museums. The ancient records are available for all to study. And they are arguably the best evidence we have for understanding the early history of Christianity.

Romans such as Pliny the Younger (ca. 110), Tacitus (ca. 115) and Suetonius (ca. 120) occasionally referenced the Christian church in their writings. They thought Christianity was an odd, insignificant superstition. Even though these writers couldn't have cared less about the Christian religion, their historical accounts still give us indisputable facts about the person of Jesus Christ. They also offer us a glimpse into events surrounding the origin of the early church.

That being said, Christians shouldn't expect too much from these ancient secular witnesses. Suetonius never came out and said, "Jesus is God's Son." Pliny the Younger never wrote, "The church's teachings are true." If these historians had made such confessions, then we couldn't accept them as the impartial secular witnesses they are. What we have here are the writings of influential Roman citizens who were concerned about the current affairs of the Roman Empire.

In the first century, Christianity was nothing more than a little-known Jewish sect in an occupied territory on the outskirts of the great Roman Empire. At that time, Christianity was of no interest to most Romans. Thus, little press was devoted to Jesus Christ and his followers. And the secular writers' comments about Christianity aren't always favorable. But despite all this, we still get our best, most objective historical evidence from the writings of these disinterested historians.

TWO POLITICIANS

Publius Cornelius Tacitus was a famous politician in the Roman Empire. He ruled toward the end of the first century. Tacitus came from a well-to-do family and studied law at the finest schools. As he progressed through the ranks, he became a popular senator, governor and consul. Tacitus was so respected that he was given the honor of speaking at the funeral of one of Rome's greatest soldiers, Lucius Verginius Rufus. Near the end of his life, Tacitus recorded a history of the Roman Empire.

In Tacitus's description of Nero's reign, he recalled a huge fire that spread across Rome. The Great Fire burned in AD 64 for five days and ultimately destroyed most of the city. Emperor Nero wanted to place the blame on someone, so he accused the Christians of arson. Nero quickly organized a sadistic crusade against all followers of Jesus Christ. And Rome publicly persecuted Christians, terrorizing them for "their hatred against mankind."[3]

During the reign of Nero, Christians were mocked, fed to wild dogs, crucified and burned alive. Tacitus graphically recounts how captured Christians were set ablaze as human torches at Nero's evening parties. The torture was so barbaric that some Roman citizens, people who deeply disliked Christians, couldn't help but feel sorry for the early church.

Tacitus was by no means a Christian. He went so far as to call Christianity a "mischievous superstition."[4] But Tacitus's lack of faith is precisely what makes him an objective witness. And Tacitus's accounts of the Great Fire and Nero's persecution of Christians give us important facts about the origin of the early church.

Tacitus was the friend of another Roman politician named Gaius Plinius Caecilius Secundus (aka Pliny the Younger). They both served in the senate together. Like Tacitus, Pliny the Younger didn't know much about the Christian religion. However, one thing was clear in Pliny's mind. First-century Christians worshipped Jesus Christ as if he were God. In his letter to Emperor Trajan, Pliny wrote:

> Having never been present at any trials of the Christians, I am unacquainted with the method and limits to be observed either in examining or punishing them...They [Christians] affirmed, however, the whole of their guilt, or their error, was, that they were in the habit of meeting on a certain fixed day before it was light, when they sang in alternate verses a hymn to Christ, as to a god.[5]

Tacitus and his friend Pliny the Younger are two of our best sources for ancient history. They clearly weren't followers of Christ, making their writings entirely objective for our purposes. And from their writings we discover some important historical facts:

1. A mysterious person named Jesus Christ lived in Israel.
2. Jesus was executed by Pontius Pilate around AD 30.
3. Immediately after the crucifixion, the Christian church formed.
4. Christians worshipped Christ as God.
5. The church grew to a sizable number before Rome's Great Fire of AD 64.
6. The Christian church continued to grow in number despite facing the terrors of persecution.

The most dependable of ancient historians always referred to Jesus as a real person. They said he lived in Israel during the first century and was executed by Pilate for various crimes. These historians never came out and said, "Jesus is the Son of God." But they did describe Jesus as a historical person who founded an odd religious sect.

Tacitus's account of Rome's Great Fire also allows us to accurately date the origin of the Christian church. At some point after Pilate executed Jesus Christ (around AD 30) and well before the Great Fire (July of AD 64), Christians started believing that Jesus Christ is the Son of God who rose from the dead. By AD 64 the church had grown large enough to draw Nero's attention. So, it's logical to infer that the Christian church began well before AD 64—immediately after Jesus's crucifixion. And at the inception of the Christian church, for some mysterious reason, followers of Jesus started worshipping Him as God.

These are the historical facts we glean from the most objective evidence we have. And history gives us facts that demand an explanation. How did Jesus's corpse disappear from his tomb? Why couldn't authorities find the missing corpse? Why did the early church believe Christ rose from the dead three days after his execution? And why did the earliest of Jesus's followers worship Him as God? To this day, the early church's faith in Christ's bodily resurrection still challenges us as history's greatest mystery.

THE COUNTERCULTURAL MOVEMENT

In the 1960s, a liberal countercultural movement emerged. Some youth of the United States preached extreme ideals about peace and love. The most animate of hippies grew long hair and wore tie-dyed shirts. Their radical message was freedom from all the restrictive norms of society. And for about a decade, the hippie movement made an undeniable countercultural statement.

Woodstock represented the height of the hippie movement. Nearly five hundred thousand people attended a three-day concert featuring the best rock and folk artists of the day. But soon after, the countercultural movement began to decline. People were murdered during a second concert at the Altamont Speedway. Charles Manson, a serial killer associated with the hippie movement, was convicted in a publicized trial. And by the end of the Vietnam War, the powerful countercultural movement fizzled.

Christians and hippies don't always have a lot in common. However, they are both members of extreme countercultural movements. Most countercultural movements are brief and fleeting. For example, the hippie movement lasted about a decade, ending with the changing of cultural trends. But the Christian movement is now two thousand years old and still strong. Even though times have changed, the Christian church has persisted.

Throughout the years, Christianity has shaped so many of our world's cultures that faith in Christ doesn't seem so countercultural anymore. But it wasn't always this way. People living in the twenty-first century can't fully appreciate how countercultural the first-century Christian church really was.

The Christian church began in an ancient Jewish culture that idealized religious intolerance. Rule breakers were kicked out of their communities. Blasphemers were tortured and stoned to death. If a Jew didn't carefully follow his or her strict religious traditions, there was a huge price to pay.

The earliest of Christians, who were primarily Jews living in Israel, rebelled against the very religious traditions they were supposed to follow. Jewish Christians were rejected by their families and disowned by their communities. All first-century Christians, both Jew and Gentile, were subjected to public humiliation and the most brutal of physical torture. They were even murdered for their faith at the hands of Jewish and Roman authorities. These Christians broke from their cultural norms and faced full-on genocide because of their unusual convictions. The fact that early Christians were persecuted so maliciously proves how countercultural their faith really was. Christianity is probably the most countercultural movement ever.

Early Christians held many countercultural beliefs. First, Christians understood the Jewish Messiah (God's chosen King of the Jews) quite differently. The following Christian beliefs about the Messiah radically opposed conventional Jewish norms:

- The King was born from a virgin.
- The King was mocked and tortured.
- The King died before establishing his earthly kingdom.
- The King visited Hell during an out-of-body experience.
- The King was resurrected from the dead.
- The King ascended into heaven.
- The King sent the Holy Spirit to believers.
- The King is God (a member of the Trinity).

These beliefs broke from the common Jewish view of the Messiah. For some mysterious reason, the early church revised many Jewish beliefs about the King of the Jews.

Second, Christians added new beliefs about the Messiah to traditional Judaism. These Christian doctrines defied all cultural norms:

- The King died as our substitute to pay the price for our sins.
- The King offers spiritual salvation through personal faith.
- The King's sacrifice makes people righteous by grace.
- The King reinterpreted parts of the old Law of Moses.
- The King cancelled other parts of the Law of Moses.
- The King established all believers as priests.
- The King made the Holy Spirit available to all people.
- The King instituted sacraments like Baptism and Communion as ways to experience grace.

These beliefs about the Messiah have no clear precedent in Judaism. Yet for some strange reason, Christians started believing such things.

Third, many Christian beliefs were deemed blasphemous by the Jewish culture at large. The following doctrines were so despicable to the Jewish society that capital punishment was a just penalty for their supporters:

- The King is God incarnate (meaning He is both God and man).
- The King should be worshipped as God.
- The King existed before the universe began.
- The King is eternal.
- The King created the universe.
- The King condemned religious traditions.
- The King will judge the world.
- The King offers the only exclusive way to salvation.

All these distinctly Christian beliefs have no recognizable roots in Judaism. They were so radically countercultural, the Jewish authorities condemned them as blasphemous. Because of this, Christians were despised, rejected, tortured and killed for their beliefs.

But through it all, something unexpected happened. The Christian movement didn't die out like other countercultural movements. And the Christian church didn't just survive. It thrived! History shows us the church miraculously grew. Despite all the natural forces discouraging faith in Jesus Christ, Christianity defied all the odds and expanded. Most countercultural movements (like the hippie movement of the 1960s) last a few years before fading. Christianity overcame the worst kind of persecution in the most intolerant of regions to become a global phenomenon. Within just 350 years after Christ's execution, Theodosius I made Christianity the official state religion of the Roman Empire. And the rest is history.

By all rational accounts, the early church's most unfavorable environment should have naturally quelled any Christian uprising. However, history proves otherwise. Something contrary to natural expectations took place. The historical evidence shows us that something "unnatural" happened. The Christian countercultural movement grew into one of the world's largest religions.

The birth and growth of the persecuted church was so unexpected and so extraordinary. There's no natural explanation for it. How could all these radical, countercultural beliefs develop within such a hostile environment? Why would early Christians reject the Jewish status quo and put their lives in danger?

Common sense can't explain how the early church's countercultural convictions formed. And there's no ordinary explanation for people choosing a persecuted life over their natural instincts for survival. Remember, in the first century, joining the Christian church meant defying one's innate desire for comfort and self-preservation. It makes no sense for people to join the Christian church and share their faith with others when they knew it exposed them to the worst kind of persecution.

So why did Christians put their lives at risk in order to promote their radical, countercultural beliefs? And where did all these countercultural beliefs come from? Our question is this: What is the best explanation for the historical fact that the Christian church emerged out of such an intolerant, dangerous climate?

Since the growth of the early church is such an "unnatural" response to persecution, it's logical to infer that something "not natural" (or supernatural) was behind the growth of the early church. If we find no human reason for the origin of this countercultural movement, then something beyond human reason is likely at work. Thus, our case for Christianity based on the most dependable of historical evidence has come to a close. And as long as our assumptions are impartial and unbiased toward supernatural explanations, it's reasonable to conclude that something supernatural was behind the birth of the Christian church.

A TALE OF TWO MIRACLES

Most every case for Christianity will contend the simplest and most plausible explanation for the early church's countercultural convictions is that some disciples actually saw the resurrected Christ. No natural explanation can adequately account for the church's unusual belief that Jesus rose from the dead. And this supernatural explanation fits with all the historical facts.

Strictly speaking, logic has nothing negative to say against a resurrection. Coming back to life is logically possible, meaning there's no obvious contradiction in the thought of a resurrected person. The notion of a resurrection is quite different from the impossible idea of a "square circle" or a "married bachelor."

Experience doesn't necessarily count against the reality of a resurrection either. Scientific knowledge is entirely compatible with a theory that God dramatically intervenes in nature every now and then. And, of course, a powerful God who created the universe could easily bring a dead person back to life.

Sure, David Hume argued that we should rely on common experience as a barometer for what is reasonable to believe. But Hume neglected to mention one simple fact. Miracles, specifically their infrequency and marvelous qualities, are precisely what we need to count as evidence demonstrating the existence of supernatural realities. Ironically, the more miraculous something is, the better it can serve as proof of the supernatural. And in light of the Grand Contradiction, Hume's secular assumptions about knowledge aren't convincing.

So how can people reasonably reject a supernatural explanation for the miraculous origin of the early church? Supposing a skeptic's reasoning is good and he or she is not getting carried away by emotions and other logical fallacies, the real cause for doubt has to do with assumptions. You see, Hume thought it was unreasonable to believe miracles occur because he first assumed "Knowledge is only about things we can see and touch." If Hume's assumptions about knowledge were different, then his logical conclusions would have been different as well.

But as we've seen in previous chapters, it's impossible to directly argue for or against any specific assumption. That would entail reasoning in a circle—depending on the very assumption in question. Nevertheless, Hume's assumptions led him into the Grand Contradiction. And we have plenty of indirect reasons to think Hume's secular assumptions are incorrect.

However, the case for Christianity doesn't end there. Christianity offers us two specific miracles to consider. The first is the physical resurrection of Jesus Christ, which historical facts substantiate. The second is the personal conviction of the Holy Spirit, which our religious experiences attest to. This Holy Spirit is what prompted early Christians to reject their natural instincts and put their lives at risk. And this same Holy Spirit is still at work today, calling us to believe and changing the lives of those who listen.

It is as Hume suggested. "The Christian religion not only was at first attended with miracles, but even at this day cannot be believed without one."[6] Ironically, what Hume meant as an insult actually establishes the reasonableness of faith in God's Word. It's true that people must have "a miracle in their own person" in order to believe. But this is exactly what we need to overcome the Grand Contradiction and finally make sense of the sound knowledge we know we have.

The work of the Holy Spirit is what frees us from all the inconsistencies and self-contradictions in our thinking. It points us in the right direction. It gives us a special belief that rightly deserves a free pass. In sum, supernatural faith in the Bible's testimony is what makes sound knowledge possible.

THE NEW WAY OF APOLOGETICS

As we consider the historical evidence for Christianity, we must always remember that our assumptions define what it means to be "rational." Keeping this in mind, the case for Christianity proves faith is completely reasonable so long as our assumptions allow for the supernatural realities found in God's Word. And we have more than enough historical evidence to logically conclude Christian faith is reasonable for those with the proper assumptions.

The real question for us is this: Are we reasoning with the best assumptions? The Grand Contradiction challenges us to indirectly question our assumptions. When we do, logic and history demonstrate this fact: Only supernatural faith in a special revelation can remove all contradictions in our thinking and give us the sound knowledge we know we have. And after we consider both the history of Western science and what world religions offer, God's Word stands tall as the best and only explanation for all our knowledge. In this way, the Bible is proven true.

But this is not the end of our story. It's only the beginning. The Holy Spirit is what creates the makings of faith within our hearts and calls us to believe. And just like our other basic intuitions, our religious intuitions tell us what is real and true. They show us who we are and how we should behave. Our basic intuitions (religious or otherwise) put us in contact with the truth.

And we must trust what they tell us. Remember, to doubt our most basic intuitions is to deny our very reality. Ancient Skeptics proved this time and time again as they demanded proofs for their assumptions, which ultimately led them to doubt the existence of the very world they lived in.

In the end, the Grand Contradiction proves what Scripture has claimed all along: "Only the fool has said in his heart, 'There is no God'" (Ps. 14:1). Christian assumptions are the best assumptions to reason with. They are the only assumptions that avoid self-refuting contradictions in our thinking and make perfect sense of the sound knowledge we know we have. Logic, history, science and Scripture are all in complete agreement here.

By focusing on the Grand Contradiction and its logical solution, Christians can now prove with clarity and decisiveness their faith is more reasonable than doubt. To learn more about the new way of apologetics, visit *thegrandcontradiction.com*.

Notes

CHAPTER ONE

1. Corey Inscoe, "In the age of Internet, thousands see mistake," *The Charlotte Observer*, February 19, 2012, http://www.charlotteobserver.com/news/local/community/south-charlotte/article9077033.html.

2. Aristotle, *Politics* (Cambridge: The Internet Classic Archives, 2009), Book 5, Part 4.

3. "Assumption," *Oxford Dictionaries Online* (Oxford University Press), www.oxforddictionaries.com.

4. Friedrich Nietzsche, *The Will to Power* (New York: Random House, 1968), 322.

5. Lewis Carroll, *Alice's Adventures in Wonderland* (Salt Lake City: Project Gutenberg, 2008), Chapter 6.

6. Plato, *Meno* (Cambridge: The Internet Classic Archives, 2009).

7. Aristotle, *Posterior Analytics* (Cambridge: The Internet Classic Archives, 2009), Book 1, Part 3.

8. Blaise Pascal, *Pensees* (London: Penguin Books, 1995), 28-29.

9. David Hume, *An Enquiry Concerning Human Understanding* (Salt Lake City: Project Gutenberg, 2003), Section 4, Part 1.

10. Aristotle, *Metaphysics* (Cambridge: The Internet Classic Archives, 2009), Book 4, Part 4.

CHAPTER TWO

1. Augustine, *Confessions* (Grand Rapids: Christian Classics Ethereal Library, 2005), Book 8, Chapter 12.

2. Pascal, *Pensees*, 28-29.

3. Ibid.

4. Ibid.

5. Quotable Quotes, *The Reader's Digest*, Vol. 37, 1940.

CHAPTER THREE

1. Alexa Miller, "The 10 Biggest Design Failures of the Last 25 Years," *Business Insider*, August 3, 2010, http://www.businessinsider.com/10-biggest-design-failures-2010-8?op=1.

2. Sky Canaves, "Shanghai Building Collapses, Nearly Intact," *Wall Street Journal*, June 29, 2009, https://blogs.wsj.com/chinarealtime/2009/06/29/shanghai-building-collapses-nearly-intact/.

3. Sextus Empiricus, *Outlines of Pyrrhonism* (New York: Oxford, 1996), Chapter 32.

4. Plato, *Meno*.

5. "Double Standard," *Oxford Dictionaries Online* (Oxford University Press), www.oxforddictionaries.com.

6. Ludwig Wittgenstein, *Philosophical Investigations* (Oxford: Basil Blackwell, 1958), 50.

7. W.K. Clifford, *Lectures and Essays* (London: Macmillan, 1879), 211.

8. Aristotle, *Posterior Analytics*, Book 1, Part 3.

9. Empiricus, *Outlines of Pyrrhonism*, Chapter 32.

10. Pew Research (see Bibliography).

CHAPTER FOUR

1. Bertrand Russell and Albert Einstein, *The Russell-Einstein Manifesto*, July 9, 1955, https://pugwash.org/1955/07/09/statement-manifesto.

2. Augustine, *Tractates on the Gospel of John* (Washington, DC: The Catholic University of America Press, 1995), Tractate 29, Section 6.

3. Hume, *Enquiry*, Section 4, Part 1.

4. Francis Bacon, *Essays, Civil and Moral* (New York: PF Collier & Son, 1914), Chapter 16.

5. W.V.O. Quine, *Pursuit of Truth* (Cambridge: Harvard University Press, 1996), 20.

CHAPTER FIVE

1. Victor Chan and the Dalai Lama, "God Is Not A Christian," *Huffington Post*, January 7, 2013, http://www.huffingtonpost.com/2013/01/07/god-is-not-a-christian-tutu-dalai-lama_n_2421553.html.

2. Hume, *Enquiry*, Section 10, Part 1.

3. David Hume, *A Treatise of Human Nature* (Salt Lake City: Project Gutenberg, 2010), Book 1, Part 4, Section 7.

4. "Rev. and Mrs. Moon," The Unification Church, http://www.unification.org/rev_mrs_moon.html.

5. *Quran*, 6:109–111,125–126.

6. *Quran*, 10:101.

7. Joseph Smith, *Doctrine and Covenants* (Salt Lake City: LDS.org, 2016), 9:7–9.

8. Gia-Fu Feng, trans., *Tao Te Ching* (New York: Vintage Books, 1972), Chapter 20.

CHAPTER SIX

1. Mark Twain, *Roughing It* (Salt Lake City: Project Gutenberg, 2006), Chapter 16.

2. Hume, *Enquiry*, Section 10, Part 1.

3. Tacitus, *The Annals* (Cambridge: The Internet Classics Archive, 2009), Book 15.

4. Ibid.

5. Pliny the Younger, *Letters* (London: William Heinemaan, 1927), Book 10, Letter 96.

6. Hume, *Enquiry*, Section 10, Part 2.

Glossary

a posteriori argument: an inductive argument based on observations and experiences that intends to show its conclusion is probably true.

a priori argument: a deductive argument based on reasoning apart from experience, which deals with certain and necessary truths about the relationships between ideas and definitions.

argument from analogy: an *a posteriori* argument that considers observed similarities to logically infer a further, unobserved similarity.

argumentum ad antiquitatem: an informal logical fallacy that appeals to a community's tradition as an indicator of truth.

argumentum ad consequentiam: an informal logical fallacy that appeals to the desired consequences of a belief for its justification.

argumentum ad passiones: an informal logical fallacy that appeals to a person's feelings and emotions to show something is true.

assumption: a foundational belief about what real and true, which is based on mysterious feelings and accepted as true without the support of arguments and evidence.

begging the question: an informal logical fallacy that takes place when the conclusion of an argument is implicitly assumed true before arguing begins.

Christian: a person who accepts Jesus Christ as Lord and Savior and trusts the Bible's testimony as his or her absolute authority on all truth.

Christian faith: the decision to trust the basic religious intuitions that compel us to believe God exists and the Bible's testimony is true.

circular reasoning: a logical fallacy in which the conclusion of an argument is also a premise within the argument.

conclusion: an intentional, reasonable inference to believe something is true based on a review of all known arguments and evidence.

doubt: the decision to question or reject basic intuitions (religious or otherwise) that compel us to believe our assumptions about truth and reality are correct.

faith: the decision to trust basic intuitions (religious or otherwise) that compel us to believe our assumptions about truth and reality are correct.

false assumption: an assumption that is untrue, inaccurate or causes a clear contradiction within our thinking.

Grand Contradiction: a self-refuting contradiction at the beginning of reasoning that forms when people committed to a secular agenda give their assumptions a free pass, thereby demonstrating they cannot follow the very rules of reasoning they seek to establish.

human reasoning: reasoning that assumes (1) it starts with natural feelings about what is real and true and (2) it deals exclusively with human thoughts about objects of our physical world.

infinite regress: the never-ending chain of arguments that forms when someone tries to directly justify an assumption with human reasoning.

knowledge: beliefs that are both true and justified by way of reasoning.

law of noncontradiction: the fundamental rule of reasoning that states something cannot both be true and untrue in the same sense at the same time.

logical fallacy: an inappropriate use of reasoning that fails to dependably establish truth and avoid falsehood.

materialism: a philosophy that asserts only physical matter exists.

natural: having to do with nature, particularly the natural causes and effects among physical objects, with no reference to the supernatural.

naturalism: a philosophy that assumes knowledge is all about natural causes and effects, thereby excluding the supernatural as either unintelligible or nonexistent.

nonreligious: having no concern for God or other spiritual matters.

philosopher: a person who reasons according to the established norms and proven standards of Western philosophy.

premise: a proposition within an argument from which a conclusion is inferred.

presuppose: to assume something is true before a reasonable demonstration is made.

rational: believing or acting according to the logical principles of Western philosophy and science.

religious experience: a personal feeling or altered state of consciousness indicating that God exists or a sacred religious text is true.

secular: a way of thinking that rejects all forms of religion.

Skeptics: members of an ancient philosophical school that critically questioned all assumptions, doubted basic intuitions about what's real and true and wound up with some absurd, self-refuting conclusions.

skeptics: people who question some of their basic instincts about truth and reality (particularly their religious intuitions) and wind up with some absurd, self-refuting conclusions.

sound knowledge: knowledge that is free from all inconsistencies and contradictions.

sound logic: logic based on fair, open-minded assumptions, which allow for a solution to the Grand Contradiction.

Bibliography

Aristotle. *Metaphysics.* Trans. W.D. Ross. Cambridge: The Internet Classics Archive, 2009. Digital file.

Aristotle. *Politics.* Trans. Benjamin Jowett. Cambridge: The Internet Classics Archive, 2009. Digital file.

Aristotle. *Posterior Analytics.* Trans. G. R. G. Mure. Cambridge: The Internet Classics Archive, 2009. Digital file.

Augustine. *Confessions.* Trans. Edward Pusey. Grand Rapids: Christian Classics Ethereal Library, 2005. Digital file.

Augustine. *Tractates on the Gospel of John.* Washington, DC: The Catholic University of America Press, 1995.

Bacon, Francis. *Essays, Civil and Moral.* Ed. Charles Eliot. New York: PF Collier & Son, 1914.

Canaves, Sky. "Shanghai Building Collapses, Nearly Intact." *Wall Street Journal.* Wall Street Journal, June 29, 2009. Web. May 5, 2014.

Carroll, Lewis. *Alice's Adventures in Wonderland.* Salt Lake City: Project Gutenberg, 2008. Digital file.

Chan, Victor and the Dalai Lama. "God Is Not A Christian." *Huffington Post.* Huffington Post, Jan. 7, 2013. Web. June 10, 2017.

Clifford, W.K. *Lectures and Essays.* Vol. 2. London: Macmillan, 1879.

Empiricus, Sextus. *Outlines of Pyrrhonism.* Trans. Benson Mates. New York: Oxford, 1996.

Feng, Gia-Fu trans. *Tao Te Ching*. New York: Vintage Books, 1972.

Hume, David. *A Treatise of Human Nature*. Salt Lake City: Project Gutenberg, 2010. Digital file.

Hume, David. *An Enquiry Concerning Human Understanding*. Salt Lake City: Project Gutenberg, 2003. Digital file.

Inscoe, Corey. "In the age of Internet, thousands see mistake." *The Charlotte Observer*. The Charlotte Observer, February 19, 2012. Web. May 5, 2014.

International Bible Society, ed. *The Holy Bible*. Grand Rapids: Zondervan, 1984.

Miller, Alexa. "The 10 Biggest Design Failures of the Last 25 Years." *Business Insider*. Business Insider, August 3, 2010. Web. May 5, 2014.

Nietzsche, Friedrich. *The Will to Power*. Trans. Walter Kaufmann. New York: Random House, 1968.

Oxford Dictionaries Online. www.oxforddictionaries.com.

Pascal, Blaise. ***Pensees***. Trans. A. J. Krailsheimer. London: Penguin Books, 1995.

Pew Research. "The Global Religious Landscape." December 18, 2012. http://www.pewforum.org/2012/12/18/global-religious-landscape-exec/.

Plato, *Meno*. Trans. Benjamin Jowett. Cambridge: The Internet Classics Archive, 2009. Digital file.

Pliny the Younger. *Letters*. Ed. E. Capps. Vol. 2. London: William Heinemaan, 1927.

Quine, W.V.O. *Pursuit of Truth*. Cambridge: Harvard University Press, 1996.

Quotable Quotes. *The Reader's Digest*. Vol. 37, 1940.

Russell, Bertrand and Albert Einstein. *The Russell-Einstein Manifesto*. July 9, 1955. https://pugwash.org/1955/07/09/statement-manifesto.

Shakir, M. H., trans. *The Quran*. Elmhurst: Tahrike Tarsile Quran, 1993.

Smith, Joseph. *Doctrine and Covenants*. Salt Lake City: LDS.org, 2016. Digital file.

Tacitus, *The Annals*. Trans. Alfred John Church and William Jackson Brodribb. Cambridge: The Internet Classics Archive, 2009. Digital file.

Twain, Mark. *Roughing It*. Salt Lake City: Project Gutenberg, 2006. Digital file.

Unification.org "Who is Reverend Moon?" http://www.unification.org/rev_mrs_moon.html.

Wittgenstein, Ludwig. *Philosophical Investigations*. Trans. G. E. M. Anscombe. Oxford: Basil Blackwell, 1958.

About the Author

C.D. Davis has over twenty-five years of experience in Christian leadership as a pastor and educator. He earned bachelor's degrees in education and business, and received a master's in theology from Talbot Theological Seminary. He loves his family and he enjoys connecting with others, exploring the depths of God's truths in community. He can be reached through email at *chris@authorcddavis.com* or by postal mail at P.O. Box 2456 Rogers, AR 72757-2456.

CPSIA information can be obtained
at www.ICGtesting.com
Printed in the USA
LVHW080357141220
674108LV00017B/985